THE MASTER ARCHITECT SERIES

EISENMAN ARCHITECTS
Selected and Current Works

THE MASTER ARCHITECT SERIES
EISENMAN ARCHITECTS
Selected and Current Works

First published in Australia in 1995 by
The Images Publishing Group Pty Ltd
ACN 059 734 431
6 Bastow Place, Mulgrave, Victoria, 3170
Telephone (61 3) 9561 5544 Facsimile (61 3) 9561 4860

National Library of Australia Cataloguing-in-Publication Data

Eisenman, Peter,1932-.
Eisenman Architects: selected and current works.

Bibliography.
Includes index.
ISBN 1 875498 21 4.
Master Architect Series ISSN 1320 7253

1. Eisenman, Peter, 1932–. 2. Eisenman Architects.
3. Architecture, American. 4. Architecture, Modern - 20th
century - United States. 5. Architects - United States.
I. Title. (Series: Master architect series).

720.92

Edited by Stephen Dobney
Designed by The Graphic Image Studio Pty Ltd,
Mulgrave, Australia
Printed by Southbank Book,
Fishermens Bend, Australia

Contents

Introduction

The Eisenman Wave
By Sanford Kwinter

It is difficult to say which is the more impressive career accomplishment: to have generated an endlessly renewed trail of agitative hypotheses over a 30-year period, or to have eschewed nearly all the comforts of consolidation—and the inevitable complacencies—afforded by conventional, repeatable "successes" such as the production of "great" buildings or the development of a signature style. In both these respects, Peter Eisenman differs not only from other architects of his own generation (it would, after all, be charitable to say that the work of his fellow "New York Five" architects has now degenerated into nothing better than mannerism), but from nearly all other architects working today.

When Eisenman's work began in the early sixties, it was, and remains to this day, a primarily *tactical* enterprise: its force from the outset was drafted from that of the enemy—classicism—but was also turned aggressively against it. The Eisenman parti has always been to deploy mobile entities such as *historical circumstances* (holocaust, Hiroshima), *situations* (death of God, transformations of domesticity and its mores) and *idea-moments* (generative grammar, structuralism, conceptualism, anti-humanism) against the ethos of established orders and places, reversing the age-old bourgeois victory of values of domain over values of time. Eisenman's task has been to develop a practice that, to borrow an expression from Foucault and Nietzsche, would come *from outside*—a new type of modernist adversarial practice to be launched from a placeless but volatile "steppe," home of disembodied fluxes, raw will to power, and the destabilizing forces of historical change. There is not now, nor has there ever been, a fixable Eisenmanian alternative architecture; tactical space after all is made up of a series of seized "occasions" (Greek *kairós*), so that the momentary triumphs that punctuate its unfolding campaign are never—indeed cannot be—stored. Like the autonomous, fluid nomad civilizations who made legendary assaults on sedentary cultures, Eisenman's practice is assembled and articulated *in movement* and in the spirit of movement. Both operate through invasion, disruption, and the release of temporarily trapped forces into free motion and recombination.

In the case of Eisenman, I will argue, these movements and abrasions unfold on three distinct yet interconnected levels: the intellectual–historical, the discursive–textual, and the material–formal. Yet despite an amazing and persistent paranoia among colleagues (primarily the dull and unfree), there exists no Eisenmanian fiefdom, no domain of concentrated "political" power, only the continuous forced convergence of "wild," impersonal idea-forces both drawn from the amorphous outside and directed at the stolid world of quiescent form. The Eisenman-effect operates like the abrasions of a wave on a beach: the parade of ideas and intellectual currents that make up our collective post-war history are made to render, through rhythmic, directed encounters, what to a humanistic tradition was once solid— both Architecture and "Man"—a shifting fluid as well.

Eisenman has never claimed to be a philosopher. It is true that he writes with seriousness and discipline, yet his texts, like his architecture, are more than anything else promiscuous material fields of collision; aggravated surfaces onto which are drawn the raw, active forces that give shape to the objects of our world. The concrete way in which ideas are here assembled (it would not be out of line to ascribe to it a barbaric creativity) elicits, to be sure, the work of Robert Smithson and certain of the American minimalists, though most of all, Eisenman's own early drawings and built work, which together are so textual and abstract that across the continuum of his practice it remains hard to say where his architecture takes place, or whether it is even primarily architecture that *is* taking place.

It has been easy to fault him for an occasional lack of rigor, yet that does not mean that such claims do not seriously miss the point. For what is important in Eisenman (and in this era of intellectual poverty and historical amnesia it merits being pointed out again) is that he is the first architect in recent history fully to take up the Futurists' challenge to conceive of all of culture—plastic as well as historical, intellectual—as a single, continuous and connected field. In the parochial, pre-Eisenmanian architectural world, it could be said that architecture was at best cultivated and intelligent; whereas today, all culture and elaborated intelligence can—at least potentially— become architecture. The ductile nature of this new field— a new type of space entirely, because it is endowed with intellectual, textual and therefore infinitely extendable dimensions—belongs to one of the greatest cultural developments of our modernity. The origins of this program can be found in Nietzsche's concept of "will to power." Nietzsche was the first to proclaim that form was but the concrete *appearance (Schein)* of invisible conflicting forces working below and across it. History, in the Nietzschean cosmos, became the history of *shaping forces*—that is, a fundamentally aesthetic phenomenon, and no longer a moral one—and this idea is one whose political implications have still today only begun to be worked out. That what is created and *said* in a "mental space" might be materially continuous with what is given shape in a domain that is entirely distinct and removed from it in nature and modality, that is, in a concrete, physical milieu; and that these two parallel but disparate types of phenomena might not only affect one another but in fact be engendered by the very same genus of forces, remains a radical epistemological claim. For how, to use Foucault's terminology, do discursive objects—discursive practices—impose their effects upon, indeed form a tissue with, concrete or non-discursive domains? Though the answer to this problem is clearly too complex to develop fully here, it is enough to say that its solution entails a resonant feature or element through which an *illocutionary* property of language (culture and expressed mental objects) connects to, and communicates with a *performative* property within the concrete or built environment.[1]

To say something in the world, as many post-war language philosophers besides Foucault claimed, is pre-eminently *to do* something. What this means in a nutshell is that linguistic and intellectual acts exist and operate by dint of their capacity actually to *change material conditions:* they program, suffuse, and in each instance, redistribute the physical world. The concept of a continuous and modulated tissue of effects that connects disparate phenomena (such as language, ideas and matter) together in a type of manifold or consistency, is a principle achievement, if not of post-war ontology, then certainly of post-war aesthetics. Language, in this emerging conjuncture, became for the first time fully and gesturally tectonic in its capacity to provoke and direct the forces of social and material assembly; the worlds of objects, institutions and buildings were increasingly seen—at least by Foucault, Deleuze and Guattari, the French inheritors of this Anglo-Saxon philosophical tradition—as hyper-dense forms of these same, fundamentally *programmatic,* milieus.

[1] The concept of the performative utterance was developed by British language philosopher John Austin. Its original formulation was meant to distinguish it from utterances which were not acts—that is, simple statements or matter-of-fact descriptions which were not actual *doings*—but only *sayings.* He originally named these latter objects *constatives,* but his entire late career was committed to withdrawing the formal distinction and extending the active, performative function to virtually all speech acts. In this extended domain, and at a level of higher nuance, he introduced the terms *illocutionary* to describe complete acts of transformation in an extra-linguistic domain (yelling 'fire' in a theater, saying 'I do' in a marriage ceremony), and *perlocutionary,* to describe acts that merely induce changes of state in the interlocutor or hearer (persuading, frightening or boring, etc.).

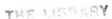 THE SURREY INSTITUTE OF ART & DESIGN

In architecture these developments found expression most fully in Eisenman where—just as in the delirious, paranoid, institutional milieus of Foucault—drawing (diagram), text and building actually came to connect with and interpenetrate one another in a promiscuous and unbroken continuum of determination and resonance. Here, all culture is *material* culture, while history, to speak like a biologist, becomes a living "excitable medium" in total intimate contact with all of its objects, shot through with, and correlated by, a propagative system of communicational waves. Every disturbance in the continuum is instantly converted into movement, registered and transmitted like an irrigating flow throughout the system.

Eisenman's earliest intellectual roots did not, of course, grow out of the traditions of continental Europe, but from those of England and America, and all too often from the narrow milieus of academic architecture and formalist aesthetics. The Eisenman of the sixties was a follower of Wittkower and Rowe (not Nietzsche and Foucault), and in the seventies, of mainstream structuralism and Chomsky's generative grammar. The search for logical or mathematically driven distributional rules appeared to be his primary interest, especially insofar as these embedded structures could be brought to the surface by rigorous operations, and there rhetorically hyper-developed at the deliberate expense of a founding "humanist" creator-subject. But of far greater importance, I would argue, even if its expression remained indirect, was Eisenman's career-long fascination with the work of Giuseppe Terragni. For Terragni's work was not, despite what most historians have argued, a rationalist, neo-Palladian grammar of static structures, but in fact a container of perpetual movement, a veritable standing wave that switched or migrated from state to state not unlike the chemical fluctuations in a Brusselator tank chemical clock.[2] This newly identified type of activity defied the calm, Platonic play of expressed orders of which these other systems were built. Indeed, Eisenman's work has always been a search (unconscious?) to find, or develop, this wave from within the classical machine.[3]

One does not need to search far to see this forcible—even hubristic—process at work, for in the early *House* projects Eisenman had already laid down the choreographic lexicon from which his later work would never fully depart. Each of these ten or so projects may be said at the outset to develop

[2] The chemical clock is a container of liquid into which a steady stream of chemicals are fed. The catalytic effects that the chemicals have on one another provoke coherent waves of color, pattern and form to appear in the solution at regular intervals. On the relation of these autocatalytic systems to architecture, see my essays "The Genius of Matter: Eisenman's Cincinnati Project," in *Peter Eisenman and Frank Gehry*, (Rizzoli, 1991), and "Maxwell's Demons and Eisenman's Conventions: Challenge Match for the 'Information' Age," *(A + U,* September 1993).

within an essentially boundary-fixed cube. Of course to say that the boundaries are fixed does not mean that they are either continuous or inviolate. They are, in fact, maniacally articulated with disruptions and deletions, crazily perforated like the program cards that drive a player piano. What is important of course is that in these experimental structures the "instrument" or resonating body, and the notational system (sheet music or program cards) are entirely coextensive with one another. There is here a very beautiful and almost mystically efficient compression of information. The structure of this type of system resembles the webways of ancestral Aboriginal dreaming tracks or songlines that articulate, like a dynamical map, virtually every physical feature of the Australian continent. No single clan or individual, of course, actually "understands" the language of any but their own, and their immediately adjacent clan's, songlines; yet by means of deeply embedded patterns and intonations (a kind of deep structure of melodic contours and phrases available to intuition though not—yet—to analysis) a continent of specified details and trajectories appears to open transparently before one like a hyper-book ever further called into being with each turn of a page.

The encounter with the Eisenman House, at least in relation to classically based architectures from which it broke, has the cultural force of this type of anti-promenade, or, in a word, of the *walkabout*. The vertigo that these houses are said to provoke is but a bourgeois symptom of the neurotic preoccupation with maps and the transcendence they are able to induce by dissociating "space" from the object-world. Rather, I propose, the houses should be seen as a deliberate ideological break from a static, time-hating space (the economy of the colonial British, or more generically, European, city), and an immersion into the fluid criss-cross of infinitely multiplied trajectorial pulses; a system where "location" is established uniquely by "events"—the perpetual "calling out" of designated material features. In the Eisenman House, as in the Australian outback, the "song" and the landscape that is sung, are materially inseparable from one another (it is impossible to say which engenders which), primarily because both are embedded in a similar kind of *deep time*. In the Aboriginal case, of course, deep time refers to the infinite conjuring

[3] That Eisenman at least consciously identified the insufficiency of these classical systems of reading, even if unable to get definitively beyond them, is irrefutable. See for example his study, "From Object to Relationship," in *Casabella*, no. 344, January 1970.

(re-enactment?) of the origins of the universe; in Eisenman, a flight into pure syntax, a renunciation of the false and distant origin. The Eisenman Walkabout House frees the origin from the one-dimensional colonial time of a fixing—a remembering and a return—and transforms it into an ever-renewable process of an engendering or *a proceeding*. The Eisenman House, in short, was never meant to furnish a home, but rather to open architecture to movement, to re-turn it toward the lost pastorality of the *nomos*.

The distribution of structure in the Houses follows this particular logic as well. Here, the impression is of a steady, corrosive propagation of "lexical features" traveling from the edge surface or envelope inward, such that the breaking up of internal surfaces may be read as square-wave interference patterns.[4] From the point of view of each House's genesis, however, (that is, its conceptual and graphic development) it actually proceeds by very simple units (squares) shifted or rotated on elastic or mobile centers. A simple nine-square grid, for example, might emit a compound beat simultaneously to the east and to the south, as in House II, producing a sixteen-square grid over which is subsequently laid a new, expanded nine-square. (We know it is a compound wave, because an "extra" square is produced at the south-east corner of the new "el".)

What has been engendered here is a type of polyrhythm whose logic is sufficiently important to all of Eisenman's work that it is worth examining a moment. The first propagation of the grid-pattern is crystal-like: it repeats the proportions (if not explicitly the units) of the original structure at the same granularity as if it were a kind of simple dendritic extension. And yes, the germinal center has shifted 45 degrees to the south-east (from $x = 1.5$, $y = 1.5$ to $x = 2$, $y = 2$), forming a kind of embedded jig or guide for the resultant standing wave.[5] Now the new, larger nine-square represents not simply an increase in the *frequency* of the structure but in its *amplitude* as well. There are two distinct, but now wedded processes: growth plus multiplication, or change in tonality, plus change in intensity or volume; and these both exist simultaneously, one inside the other. The effect is a series of nervous, reversible phase shifts that travel through the system, generating vibratory phenomena of varying period across

---

[4] Square waves are rectangle-shaped energy pulses that oscillate regularly between two values but whose amplitude remains constant between jumps.

[5] A standing wave is sometimes known as a stationary wave. It is created by the superimposition of a reflected wave on top of an incident wave that is propagating through a vibrating medium. The incident wave is "processed" at the medium's boundaries where either some or all of the wave's energy (and therefore its structure) is returned back toward its source so that an interference pattern is created, distributing nodes and antinodes across the transmitting surface. The energy or information, to underscore my main theme, propagates endlessly while the pattern remains, if not the same, at least highly stable.

every surface. And just as lines are moved in the initial stages in order to extend surfaces, to multiply internal frequencies, and to recalibrate amplitudes, surfaces and volumes too are set into motion. Again the operation is relatively simple: a surface or volume is permitted to slide along a jig, to "shed" geometry as it sweeps and frays, and to absorb the resultant disturbances and interferences by stretching and multiplying. Yes, these are cool, mechanical operations, but they produce fluid patterns of restless stabilization. The difference between this type of compositional system and the familiar classical ones is that here order is sought, and produced, far from, rather than close to, equilibrium. Eisenman-space has demonstrably always been approaching the algorithmic, the active, and the living.

In an Eisenman work, structure always emanates from an initial pattern that is knocked away from equilibrium. The disturbance then travels, reaches a limit, then turns back toward itself to form a self-interfering wave. The structural information, or modulus, proceeds in discrete steps along the wave, coming to a momentary rest at the next, and then at each subsequent beat. Each of these beats may be conceived of spatially as marking the floor of a basin or the trough of a sine wave. But the passage of this flickering modulus also *rakes the space*, articulating and disarticulating all that lies along its path: be it the real substance deposited according to the logic of another propagative center, or simply the ghost memories of a previous or future wave that has, or soon will have, passed through the synapse. The raking process links the discrete residues to the dynamic standing wave that subtends them. Such a system is no different from the sand shapes seen in Chladni figures—the elaborate regular patterns formed on resonating metal plates when a standing wave has been applied to them. Thus the continuous, one is lead confidently to conclude, exists even within the (homeo)static.

The entire Eisenman project, one could say, is lodged within the specific Modernist paradox: the theory of *continua*. This concerns the manner according to which energy (photons, electrons, etc.) may travel in waves, yet once located, arrested, and fixed in position, can express itself only as a particle. It was in Terragni that Eisenman first confronted the mechanics of this paradox—a kind of quantum indeterminacy *where the particle and the wave coexist within one another* prior to the analytical "wave function collapse" described by the equations of Erwin Schrödinger and Louis de Broglie, that splits them definitively apart. De Broglie posited the concept of "matter waves" in 1923, while C.J. Davisson confirmed the hypothesis in two separate experiments in 1925 and 1927, the same years in which Terragni had begun to produce his first significant work.[6] Eisenman always sought to articulate textually the intuited paradox in Terragni's work with the particular language model of analysis that obsessed and inspired the work of most of his generation, but through which it simply could not be expressed.[7] Yet Eisenman's drawings and works nonetheless always possessed an *excessive* part that moved—silently and even unconsciously—beyond the limits of the analytical paradigm. It is here, in this excessive and unconscious space beyond the reach of reductionist analytics, that one finds the full blooming of the Eisenman effect and the Eisenman wave.

On virtually every level, Eisenman's impact on architectural culture has been to render continuous and active what was previously separate and inert. It is always the introduction of a continuum into a discrete and disjunctive milieu that unleashes the processes of communicative disruption. But here is an anticlassicism of a very specific kind; one that is nowhere more obviously—or furtively—apparent than in Eisenman's idiosyncratic use of script. In the typographical world, the roman forms—discrete, upright letters that mime the bombastic orders and monumentality of stone—are, in Eisenman's hand at once ridiculed and mobilized by the single, fluid line that renders the same letters in a unique, continuous—almost exaggerated—cursive stroke. Here, the cursive form seizes power, visibly forcing the roman form to submit to its rule in a microdrama that throws all of Eisenman's plastic and graphic work into newly clear relief. For beyond the polysemantism that the linguistic Eisenman imagined himself to be producing, beyond the polyresonance of multiple geometric orders that the formalist Eisenman conceived himself to be orchestrating, there lies another, perhaps more salient, Eisenman, though for that all the more hidden, even to himself: the Eisenman of movement, of the cursive form, of the continuous field, and of the propagating wave.

[6] De Broglie was awarded a Nobel Prize for this work in 1929.

[7] Peter Eisenman, *Giuseppe Terragni*, (unpublished).

Like the photon itself, Eisenman has always been a creature of two intimately linked but irreconcilable phases: when he speaks and thinks about what he does he belongs to the classical particle world, but when drawing pen across paper, and moving ideas across the cultural spectrum, he forms a formidable wave. And yet it is perhaps well that this is so; because for the new generations emerging today, systematically removed from the intellectual turbulence out of which both the Modern and the Eisenmanian projects emerged, it is the built objects and the drawn artifacts that will continue to sing, in all their gritty, assiduous and mute refinement, in all their plastic and visual *excess,* about the new world to which Eisenman's particular brand of Modernist rhetoric itself could never explicitly speak, but to which the multiple risks and forms that mark his 30-year career unfailingly give place.

Selected and Current Works

House I

Design/Completion 1967/1968
Princeton, New Jersey
Mr and Mrs Bernard M. Barenholz
3,000 square feet
Wood frame
Exterior: painted wood panels
Interior: painted wood and brick panels

This house symbolizes the new family structure of a professional couple that must occasionally live apart because of their separate work schedules.

The design relates the miniature scale of their toys to the normal scale of the individual. This creates a series of transitions from overly large to excessively small, where the individual must stoop to look at the toys. The new house seems to be a large toy next to the existing house.

1

2 3

18

1   View from the south-east
2   Axonometric study sketch: view from the north-east
3   Axonometric study sketch: view from the south-west
4–6 Ground level study sketches
7–9 Upper level study sketches

10

11

12

13

14

15

16

17

18

19

20

21

22

23

24

25

26

27

House II

Design/Completion 1969/1970
Hardwick, Vermont
Mr and Mrs Richard Falk
2,000 square feet
Wood frame
Exterior: painted wood panels
Interior: painted wall board

The house is situated on the highest point
of a 100-acre site with panoramic views on
three sides which extend for 20 miles.

The design simulates the presence of trees
and hedges, which are non-existent on the
barren hilltop, through a sequence of
columns and walls. These architectural
elements frame and focus the view and
ensure a transition from extroverted
summer activities to the introverted
security of the winter fireplace.

1

2

3

4

5

6

7

8

9

11

12

13

10

16

17

14

15

18

19

20

21

23

24

22

House III

Design/Completion 1969/1971
Lakeville, Connecticut
Mr and Mrs Robert Miller
3,500 square feet
Wood frame
Exterior: painted wood panels
Interior: painted wall board

House III is the third in a series of investigatory projects that search for the form–meaning relationship in architecture. The owner enters the house as an intruder in an attempt to regain possession and, consequentially, destroys the unity and completeness of the architectural structure. The interior void of the structure acts as both background and foil, as a conscious stimulant for the activity of the owner.

No longer concerned with imposing some preconceived idea of good taste, the house works dialectically to stimulate the owner to a new kind of participation.

1

2

1 View from the east
2 Axonometric
3 View from the east
4 First level plan
5 Second level plan

3

4

5

6

7

8

9

10

11

House IV

Design 1971
Falls Village, Connecticut
3,000 square feet

In House IV, a physical environment has been produced which is semantically and culturally diminished or more neutral. To do this, the conceptual structure has been overstressed to give it primacy over the perceptual or traditional structure of understanding an architecture.

This house is an attempt to produce a physical environment which could be generated by a limited set of formational and transformational rules. Spatial relationships are in the syntactic domain of architecture and, since our present knowledge of the nature of these relationships is rather imprecise, it is difficult to code an architecture or produce a precise set of transformational rules.

1

2   3

4

5

6

7

8

9

10

11

12

13

14

15

16

17

House VI

Design/Completion 1972/1975
Cornwall, Connecticut
Mr and Mrs Richard Frank
2,000 square feet
Wood frame
Exterior: painted wood panels
Interior: painted wall board

This weekend house on a small
rural site in north-western Connecticut
provides the owners—a photographer
and his wife—with a sensuous and playful
environment, full of continuously
changing light, shadows, color, and
textures. The house is a studio landscape,
providing an abstract background for
the photography of still life and people.
In doing so, the house and its occupants
become part of a series of daily "living
portraits."

1

2

3

4

5

6

8

9

10

7

11

13

14

12

15

16

17

22

23

18

19

24

20

21

House X

Design 1975
Bloomfield Hills, Michigan
Mr and Mrs Arnold Aronoff
3,000 square feet

This private residence is situated on a large, wooded, sloping site, adjacent to a country club. It is surrounded by a swimming pool, a tennis court and a summer house. The design uses the slope of the land in such a way that the natural landscape runs through the house, splitting it into four quadrants and reducing its scale.

1

2

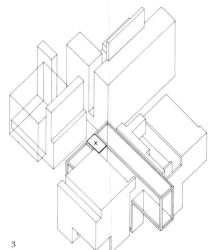

3

1   Model (Scheme G), view from the north-east
2   Axonometric diagram showing east–west arm of glass el pushing into
     north-east quadrant
3   Axonometric diagram showing perimeter frame of glass el
4   Axonometric diagram showing center as point of intersection
5   Axonometric diagram showing introduction of square gridding in glass el
6   Axonometric diagram showing glass el pulled away from north-east
     quadrant and pushing into north-west quandrant
7   Plan diagram of two north quadrants showing glass el pulled

4

5

6

7

8

9

10

11

14

15

12

13

16

17

18

19

20

21

22

23

24

25

26

27

Cannaregio Town Square

Design 1978
Venice, Italy
Municipal Government of Venice

This project is derived from an architecture that invents its own site and program. Rather than reproducing an existing Venice, it constructs another, fictitious Venice. The grid of Le Corbusier's Venice Hospital is continued as a structure over the site. This grid marks a series of voids which act as metaphors for man's displacement from his position as the centered instrument of measure. Architecture becomes the measure of itself.

The objects in this landscape are variations of House 11a, shown at different scales. The small object is too small to provide shelter, but raises the question of whether it is a house or a model of a house. The middle object contains the smaller object inside it, while the large object is twice the size of the middle object.

1

9

10

13

14

11

12

House El Even Odd

Design 1980
Palo Alto, California

House El Even Odd begins with an
el-shaped axonometric object as its initial
condition of reality. Two axonometric
transformations then take place, allowing
it to appear simultaneously as a three-
dimensional object, an axonometric
projection, and a plan. The object is then
turned upside-down and placed below
ground, so that the element that seems
to be a plan is actually a roof. A smaller
el-shaped volume which fits within the
cut-out of the larger one is suspended in
space, allowing two possible readings.
A third and smaller volume, concentric to
the first, suggests the same two readings.
The three nesting els together ask, which
is the actual size, and which is the model
of the actual size?

1

2

3

4

5

6

7

8

9

10

11

F O L D I N G S   T R A C I N G S   S C A L I N G S   G R I D D I N G S

Madison Components Plant

Design/Completion 1981/1982
Madison, Indiana
Cummins Engine Company
326,000 square feet
Steel and concrete block

This industrial building was designed to house a turbo-charger and diesel engine components manufacturing process. The focus of the design was to create a well ordered and smoothly functioning interior layout: a working environment which ensured worker safety and enhanced productivity.

The manufacturing plant was designed as a single-story rectangular building with a dramatic, angled skylight running its length. In the master plan, the existing plant and new administration center are surrounded by the industrial space to allow manufacturing activities to be viewed in all varieties of light without glare off the machinery.

1

1   Presentation model, view from above
2   Presentation model, view from the south-east

2

3

4

5

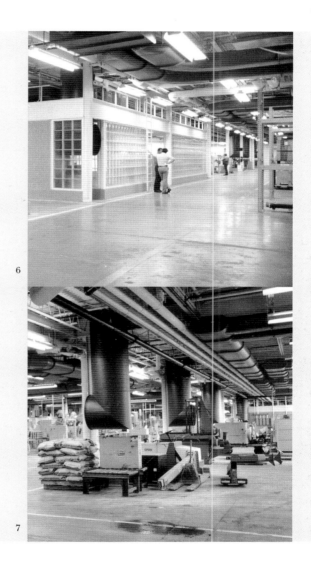

6

7

IBA Social Housing

Design/Completion 1981/1985
Berlin, Germany
Hauert Noack, GmbH & Company
50,000 square feet
Concrete frame
Stucco and metal panels

This apartment block is intended not only to help meet the pressing need for housing in Berlin, but also to commemorate the events that have taken place around the site.

This project is designed for social (low-income) housing on a corner site in Berlin, located on the block adjacent to the former Berlin Wall and Checkpoint Charlie. It is the first phase of a two- or three-phase project which will eventually cover the entire block.

The design, in addition to meeting the very restrictive functional and financial requirements for social housing in Berlin, responds in a unique way to two general architectural problems: context and symbolism.

1

1 View from the south-west
2 View from the south
3 Axonometric, view from the south-west
4 Concept sketch

2

3

4

5

6

5 View from the south
6 Facade study
7 Block plan
8 Second level plan
9 Basement level plan

7

8

9

10

11

10   South elevation, view from the south-east
11   West elevation
12   View from the south-west
13   North elevation
14   South elevation

12

13

14

15

16

17

18

19

20

21

Travelers Financial Center

Design/Completion 1983/1986
Hempstead, New York
Fair Oaks Development/Schottenstein Properties
235,000 square feet
Steel frame
Glass and aluminum curtain wall

The design for this 10-story office building on Long Island consists of eight floors of office space, with retail facilities on the ground floor and a lower level containing a private dining area and building services.

The building demonstrates a plasticity of form and surface not ordinarily associated with curtain-wall office buildings. This "glass box" is effectively broken into several different readings by a number of shifts in the plans and elevations. The two geometries of the site are encapsulated in the small-scale interplay of the wall, surface and grid in the ceilings, floor and walls of the main lobby level.

1

2

1 View from the south-west
2 South elevation
3 Axonometric of lobby ceiling, view from below
4 North elevation
5–6 Detail views from the south
7 View from the west

3

4

8

9

10

11

12

13

14

Firehouse for Engine Company 233
and Ladder Company 176

Design/Completion 1983/1985
Brooklyn, New York
City of New York
13,500 square feet
Steel frame
Glazed and non-glazed block and aluminum panels

The building's design responds to its urban site, where an elevated rail line marks a shift in grid patterns, by incorporating these two grids within the structure. This two-story firehouse contains fire-fighting equipment, battalion chief's offices, company offices, and sleeping accommodation.

The structural roof beam members of the superimposed grid contain red laser lights that symbolically illuminate the structure at night. In addition, a beacon of red light shines out when the fire engines are on-call.

1

1 View from the west
2 First level plan
3 Second level plan
4 Detail view from the north-west
5 Interior view

4

5

2

3

6

7

8

9

12

13

10

11

Fuller/Toms Loft

Design/Completion 1984/1987
New York, New York
Emily Fuller and Newby Toms
4,800 square feet
Wood floor, wallboard walls and ceiling,
sliding wood doors

The ideas for this project are twofold:
first, to explore the question of scale;
second, to explore the question of an
internal insertion.

The site for this project is a loft in Lower
Manhattan. The space is essentially a
rectangular parallelepiped with a
proportion of 40 to 100. The short side
faces Broadway, a diagonal in the
orthogonal street grid of New York.
The idea is to insert a foreign body into
the existing context in such a way as to
produce a disorienting relationship
between old and new. The intersection of
the two geometries produces a condition
in which neither geometry is dominant,
thereby displacing and destabilizing
conventional devices for orientation.

1

1 Living/dining room
2–3 Axonometric views

2

3

4

7

8

5

6

Selected and Current Works

Romeo and Juliet Castles

Design 1985
Verona, Italy

The program for this project was to present the dominant themes of the stories of Romeo and Juliet in architectural form at the site of the two castles. There are three important versions of the story which were taken as the basis of the architectural "program."
Each narrative is characterized by three structural relationships: division (the separation of the lovers/the balcony); union (the marriage of the lovers/the church); and their dialectical relationship (the togetherness and apartness of the lovers/Juliet's tomb). The project responds to fundamental cultural changes that have taken place in the last century, by using an architectural discourse that is founded in a process called scaling.

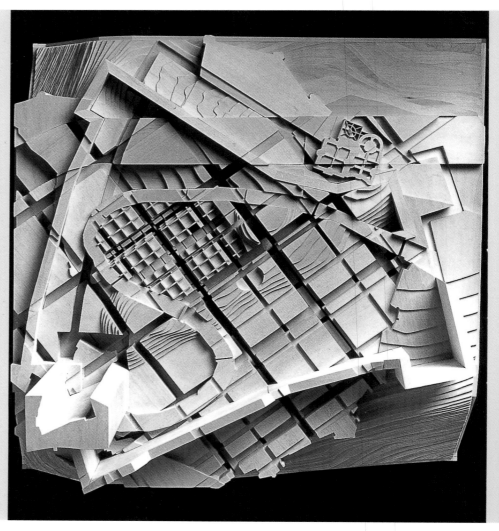

1

1   Presentation model, view from above
2   Axonometric
3–4 Plans

3

4

2

5

7

8

6

Tokyo Opera House

Design 1985
Tokyo, Japan
City of Tokyo

This competition entry for the design of the new National Theater of Japan includes three theaters (a black-box theater, a 1,000-seat performance space, and an 1,800-seat opera house), a rehearsal space, office space, and underground parking.

This project attempts to establish an analogical relationship between the proposed site of a new center for culture and the old center of culture in Tokyo, which was traditionally the Noh Theater, located in the courtyard of the Emperor's realm. To symbolize this, a series of analogous relationships between old and new were established that ultimately refer back to the Emperor's realm in Kyoto.

1

1 Presentation model, view from the west
2 Ground level plan
3 Small theater level plan
4 Medium theater level plan

5

6

11

12

7

8

9

10

Biocentrum

Design 1987
Frankfurt am Main, Germany
J.W. Goethe University
350,000 square feet

This expansion of existing biotechnology research laboratories and support spaces was approached by considering the foundations of biology as an analogy for development of the scheme. DNA is used as a model of a logical sequence with infinite possibilities for expansion, change, and flexibility. Within this model, the design of the laboratory incorporated certain key technical design goals: providing a safe environment which protects the researchers and other building occupants from the various hazards encountered; heating, ventilating and air conditioning design which reduces the hazards of cross-contamination of experiments, and the spread of odors, toxic materials and other foreign agents.

1

2

3

4

5

6

7

8

9

9　Presentation model, view from the south-east
10　Ground level plan
11　First level plan
12　Axonometric, view from the north-east
13　Concept diagrams

12

13

10

11

14

15

16

17

La Villette

Design 1986
Parc de La Villette, Paris, France
Establissement Public du Parc de la Vilette
4,300 square feet

Parc de la Villette is a study of time—past, present, and future—and a questioning of representation in architecture. It replaces the actual conditions of time, place, and scale with analogies of these conditions. While the site exists in the present, it is also made to contain allusions to the present, the past, and the future. Analogies are made between the conditions that existed at the site in 1867, when an abattoir occupied the site; in 1848, when the site was covered by the city walls; and at the present, the time of Bernard Tschumi's La Villette project. The resultant ambiguous nature of time and place suggests an architecture that does not exist only in the present, but reverberates, suggesting an ever-increasing set of references.

1

1 Presentation drawing, plan of scheme for site 3
2 Presentation drawing, axonometric of scheme for site 1
3 Plan, second scheme
4 Presentation model, second scheme

2

4

3

5

6

9

10

7

8

University Art Museum

Design 1986
Long Beach, California
University of California, Long Beach
67,500 square feet

The master plan and museum design is
the result of a history given to the project,
compiled from a series of significant dates:
the settlement of California in 1849; the
creation of the campus in 1949; and the
rediscovery of the museum in 2049.

The building consists of four major
exhibition spaces: an audiovisual
installation gallery, a black-box theater/
auditorium, a cafe, a conference space,
a library, administrative offices and storage
areas, and a series of exterior terraced
sculpture courtyards. The arboretum will
contain a 2-acre artificial pond, botanical
gardens, terraces, and seating areas. An
elevated walkway provides a link between
the northern and southern portions of the
arboretum.

1

2

1 Presentation model, view from the west
2 Ground level plan
3 Site plan
4 Roof plan
5–6 Presentation models, view from above

5

6

3

4

FOLDINGS TRACINGS SCALINGS GRIDDINGS

7

8

11

12

9

10

Progressive Corporation Office Building

Design 1986
Cleveland, Ohio
Progressive Corporation

The site was developed from the superposition of aspects of the geographical history of the state of Ohio and the city of Cleveland: the 18th century boundary of the Connecticut Western Reserve; the 1903 Daniel Burnham plan; and the Greenville Trace—surveys of the state carried out simultaneously from the north and south. These elements were altered in size and superposed on one another. All of the conditions, fictitious and real, artificial and natural, exist simultaneously in this reinvented site. The buildings sit on the site like huge chisels, breaking the pieces open to reveal the many-faceted layers of their history.

1

1   Presentation model, view from the north-west
2   Site plan
3   Axonometric, view from the west

2

3

4

6

7

5

Wexner Center for the Visual Arts and Fine Arts Library

Design/Completion 1983/1989
Columbus, Ohio
The Ohio State University, State of Ohio
140,000 square feet

Instead of selecting any of the obvious building sites on the campus, a site was created by locating the Center between several proposed sites and existing buildings. This can be described as a non-building, an archaeological earthwork whose essential elements are scaffolding and landscaping.

The scaffolding consists of two intersecting three-dimensional gridded corridors which link existing buildings with the new galleries and arts facilities. One part of scaffolding is aligned with the Columbus street grid, the other with the campus grid, so the project both physically and symbolically links the campus with the city beyond. The Center acts as a symbol of art as process and idea.

1

1 View from the south
2 Site plan
3 Ground level plan

2

3

4

5

4   View from the south-east
5   Conceptual sketch
6   Section through lobby and offices, view from the south
7   Section through upper lobby and moat, view from the south
8   Scaffolding, detail view from the south-east
9   Scaffolding, detail view from the south

10

11

12

13

14

15

16

19

20

17

18

Selected and Current Works

Carnegie Mellon Research Institute

Design 1988
Pittsburgh, Pennsylvania
Carnegie Mellon University
85,000 square feet

Eisenman Architects was selected to develop a master plan for the Pittsburgh Technology Center and design a new facility for the Carnegie Mellon Research Institute. The design had to address the "knowledge revolution," and represent Pittsburgh's revitalization as the first post-industrial city.

The fundamental structure for this development is the "Boolean cube," a geometric model for computer processing. Each building is made up of pairs of cubes. Each pair contains two solid cubes and two frame cubes corresponding to office and laboratory modules. Each pair can be seen as containing the inverse of the other as solid and void.

1

2

3

4

5

6

7

8

9

10

11

12

13

14

15

16

GRIDDINGS SCALINGS TRACINGS FOLDINGS

CMRI
OOF LEVEL SITE PLAN

17

18

19

20

21

22

23

Guardiola House

Design 1988
Cadiz, Spain
Mr Javier Guardiola Sr
1,200 square feet

This house can be seen as the manifestation of a receptacle in which traces of logic and irrationality are intrinsic components of the object/place. It exists between the natural and the rational, between logic and chaos; the arabesque. It breaks the notion of figure/frame, because it is figure and frame simultaneously. Its tangential el-shapes penetrate three planes, always interweaving. These fluctuating readings resonate in the material of this house which, unlike a traditional structure of outside and inside, neither contains nor is contained. It is as if it were constructed of a substance which constantly changes shape.

1

2

3

4

5

6

7
8

9

11

12

10

13

15

18

19

16

17

Guardiola House   135

Aronoff Center for Design and Art

Design/Completion 1988/present
Cincinnati, Ohio
University of Cincinnati
273,000 square feet

Design disciplines must assume a more important role in our media-dominated age of information than ever before. The Aronoff Center for Design and Art is programmed to be a model for this kind of leadership. For this project, we had to reconceptualize what a building has to be in order to house such inventive, contemporary activity.

The vocabulary of the building derives from the curves of the land forms and the chevron forms of the existing building; the dynamic relationship between these two forms organizes the space between them. We worked with the students, faculty, administrators, and friends of the College so that the building was an evolutionary process of work which everyone can say "was created by us."

1

2

3

4

5

6

7

8

9

10

12

13

11

14

15

16

17

18

19

20

21

22
23

28

29

24

25

26

27

Koizumi Sangyo Office Building

Design/Completion 1988/1990
Tokyo, Japan
Koizumi Sangyo Corporation
43,000 square feet

In the West, the concept of place (*topos*) has always been pre-eminent. Less important, but latent or repressed in this topos, has been the concept of *atopia*, or no place. Tokyo can be seen as embodying a concept of atopia lying with topos. This project proposes that this "lying within" can be seen as another order, another potential structure. These ideas have always been a part of Japanese thought: the Japanese word *ma* stands for the notion of "the space between," and *ku* for "no place." In this project, the idea was not to build the place, but to build a place between. The project deals with the idea of imprint—the former presence of place—and trace—the absence of place—as the major components of any space.

1

144

1 View from the east
2 Ground level plan
3 Showroom, ground level plan
4 View of exhibition gallery from the north-east
5 View of showroom from the west

6

6   View from the north-east
7   Showroom, third level plan
8   Fifth level plan
9   Facade detail
10 View of exhibition gallery from the north-east

9

10

7

8

11

14

15

16

12

13

17

20

21

18

19

Siena Bank Master Plan

Design 1988
Siena, Italy
Monte Paschi Bank/Siena Chamber of Commerce
60,000 square feet

The program for the Siena Bank Competition required the design of an office building, parking garage, and bus terminal, while unifying two adjacent piazzas on an elevated site in the center of this historic hill town. We examined the site for traces of political and geographical histories, looking for similarities in form which might lead to a different understanding and interpretation of the town and its past.

By moving the old city wall down and moving the line of the oval up to the level of the piazza, a link was created between the levels of the city, allowing the upper level to display the full range of its archaeological nature.

1

1   Presentation massing model
2   Massing plan
3   Site section EE

2

3

4 Presentation building model, view from the north-west
5 331 elevation level plan
6 Site section FF
7 331 elevation level plan
8 Roof level plan

5

6

7

8

GRIDDINGS SCALINGS TRACINGS FOLDINGS

Greater Columbus Convention Center

Design/Completion 1989/1993
Columbus, Ohio
Greater Columbus Convention Center Authority
530,000 square feet

The design for the Greater Columbus Convention Center is simultaneously suggestive of the railyards that once occupied the site, nearby highway ribbons, and overlays of delicate fiber optic cables that represent the information age. It reflects High Street's traditionally narrow structures with articulated facades that have been extruded away from the street.

The design also solves one of the most persistent problems in convention center design—diagrammatic clarity. Differences in forms clearly distinguish the various exhibition spaces and parts of the concourse. The strengths of the scheme are accomplished without relying on unsatisfying quotations from Columbus's past, or images typically found in "generic" convention halls.

1

2

3

4

5

6

7

8

9

10

11

2

13

14

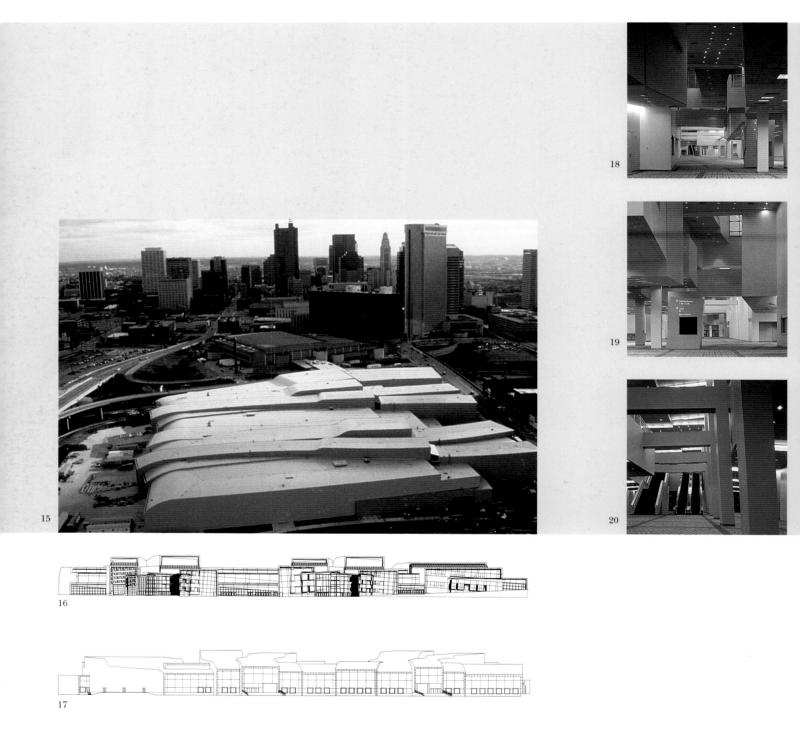

15

16

17

18

19

20

21

22

23

24

25

26

28

29

27

Banyoles Olympic Hotel

Design 1989
Banyoles, Spain
Consorci Pel Desenvolupament de la Vila Olimpica
82,000 square feet

In our project for a hotel at the site of the 1992 Olympic rowing events in Banyoles, the building is no longer a primary form—a single metaphysical enclosure. Instead, there are exponential torsions and phase shifts which characterize the line. This produces a building of richness and complexity, while at the same time preserving the simple autonomy and replication of bedroom units. It is also a building which is also part landscape.

Equally the "interior" space of the building is no longer merely the static lobby-corridor-room stacking of the traditional hotel. Instead, there is a sliding and a slipping found in the possibility of the form of the line which creates another condition of interior/exterior space.

1

2

1   Presentation site model, aerial view
2   Site plan
3   Concept diagram, base bar and landscape registration
4   Concept diagram, rowing displacement and bar tilt
5   Concept diagram, imprint and overlap
6–7   Longitudinal section, partial

8

9

10

11

12

13

14

15

16

17

18

Cooper Union Student Housing

Design 1989
New York, New York
The Cooper Union
50,000 square feet

This project breaks down traditional aspects of classical monumentality and replaces them with a freer, richer, more playful massing which has no defined frame, no single axis, and no conformity of material to shape or form to function.

The Cooper Union is the "home" for students and the portal through which they venture into the life of the city. Thus, our project addresses both symbolic and functional aspects. It begins with private units for two people, then facilities for four to six people, and then loft-style duplex living areas for 16 to 32 students. The organization provides for both community and privacy, flexibility and order, breaking down the scale of a large building into recognizable human units.

1

2

1   Ground level plan
2   Third level plan
3   Presentation model, view from the north
4   Eighth–tenth level plan
5   Roof level plan

3

OPEN TO BELOW

4   5

6

7

8

9

10

11

12

Groningen Music-Video Pavilion

Design/Completion 1990
Groningen, The Netherlands
Groningen City Festival
2,000 square feet

As part of the 1990 Groningen City Festival, Eisenman Architects was commissioned to build one of several satellites to the municipal museum. Our project is based on the idea that the new video technology is revolutionizing the notion of the moving image. The structure of our pavilion is based on an analysis of the way a video image is produced on a picture screen. Visitors to our pavilion follow a path which is analogous to that of a scanning beam's path on a video screen. Thus, the visitors become part of the medium itself, passing in front of viewing screens and continually crossing through images, shifting position to form images in different ways, and running interference. The project alludes to the traditional auditorium in its sloping floors.

1

2   3   4

5   6   7

8

9

10

11

12

13

14

15

Nunotani Office Building

Design/Completion 1990/1992
Tokyo, Japan
Nunotani Company Ltd
40,000 square feet

The land mass of Japan is constantly subjected to earthquake activity, and the Nunotani building is seen as a metaphoric record of these continuous waves of movement. Simultaneous to this analogy, the project represents an attempt to rethink the symbolism of the vertical office building, first by producing a building that is not metaphorically skeletal or striated, but rather made up of a shell of vertically compressed and translated plates; and second, by producing an image somewhere between an erect and a "limp" condition.

The building consists of studio and office spaces, a multimedia presentation room, library, cafeteria, CAD workrooms and traditional Japanese resting rooms.

1

1 Exterior, view from the north-east
2 Site plan
3 Roof plan
4 Exterior, view from the east
5 Exterior, view from the south

2

3

4

5

6

7

8

9

10

11

12

15

16

17

13

14

18

19

22

23

20

21

Atocha 123 Hotel

Design 1990
Madrid, Spain
Sociedad Belga de los Pinares de el Paular
47,000 square feet

This 92-room, four-star hotel was designed for the corner of Atocha and Alameda streets in downtown Madrid. With depths and heights established by zoning requirements, a series of diagrams was developed to derive the building form. First, bars were laid out parallel to Atocha, with a depth of one room, a height of two and a half floors, and separated by the width of a corridor. Second, bars of the same depth, height, and separation were repeated parallel to Alameda. Third, the bars parallel to Alameda were spread exponentially along the site until parallel to Prado, and the bars parallel to Atocha spread perpendicular to Prado. These manipulations produced a building form that responds to the richness of its urban environment.

1

2

1   Interior, lobby perspective
2   Site plan
3–4 Concept diagram, Cartesian line
5–6 Concept diagram, rotation and overlay plan
7–8 Concept diagram, exponential translation plan
9   Sixth level plan
10   Ground level plan

3

4

5

6

7

8

9

10

11

12

15

16

17

13

14

Selected and Current Works

Rebstockpark Master Plan

Design 1990
Frankfurt, Germany
Advanta Management, AG/Dieter Bock
5,000,000 square feet

The Rebstockpark Master Plan reassesses the idea of a static urbanism; the temporal dimension of the present becomes an important aspect of the past and the future. This reading might reveal other conditions which may have always been immanent in the urban fabric.

Framed by a segment of the Mercator grid, the Rebstockpark Master Plan floats within a rectilinear container to obscure the residual position it occupies along Frankfurt's third green belt. By compressing the large grid segment onto the site perimeter and similarly compressing the small-scale grid onto the close site, contingent readings emerge as the two site figures fold and unfold, each relative to its expanded position.

1

1   Site plan
2   Concept diagram, superposition of net
3   Concept diagram, transformation of net
4   Concept diagram, folded net
5   Concept diagram, typological fabric
6   Concept diagram, building typology
7   Concept diagram, folded typology

2

3

4

5

6

7

8

9

194

12

13

10

11

14

FOLDINGS TRACINGS SCALINGS GRIDDINGS

17

18

19

15

16

Alteka Office Building

Design 1991
Tokyo, Japan
Alteka Corporation
30,000 square feet

A paradigmatic city of accumulation, juxtaposition, and compression, Tokyo is an index of contingent, tentative relations and new, complex urban realities. Our project suggests another relationship to the city. Caught between the traditional city fabric and the Jigamae, the site suggests a building defined by fluctuation, where the object takes place in a continuum of variation. Thus, the building does not correspond to a spatial mold, but to a temporal modulation that implies a continual variation of the matter and a perpetual development of the form. The typological el frees its folds from their subordination to the finite body, emerging from the context to fold and unfold.

1

198

2

3

4

5

6

7

8

9

12

13

10

11

Emory Center for the Arts

Design 1991
Atlanta, Georgia
Emory University
160,000 square feet

The Center for the Arts at Emory University accommodates four major performance spaces (a 1,100-seat music hall, and a recital hall, studio theater, and cinema each seating 200), and is designed to be a national and international center for scholarship and performance in the fields of theater, music, and film.

The four performance halls are linked by an expansive, multi-level lobby traversing the length of the building and functioning as a link between the campus boundary and a new open-air amphitheater. Academic spaces are located to the east of the lobby over the parking garage, and rehearsal and support space is provided adjacent to the performance halls.

1

2

1 Presentation model, view from the north-west
2 Site plan
3 Concept diagram
4 945 level plan
5 977 level plan
6 964 level plan

3

4

5

6

7

8

9

10

11

12

13

14

15

16

17

18

19

20

22

21

Max Reinhardt Haus

Design 1992
Berlin, Germany
Advanta Management, AG/Dieter Bock
1,000,000 square feet

The dominant character of the Max Reinhardt Haus is both symbolic and recreational. Named for the famous German theatrical entrepreneur, it occupies the site of his former *schauspielhaus*. Its symbolism is intended to be forward rather than backward-looking, combining the best of what is German with a symbolic vision of the future. Its program is representative of Reinhardt's energy and vision: a present-day media center. Almost by definition, the building has to assume a "prismatic" character; that is to say, it needs to fold into itself—but also open itself out to—an infinite, always fragmentary, and constantly changing array of metropolitan references and relationships.

1

2

3

4

5

7

6

8

10

11

9

12

13

14

15

16

17

18

19

20

22

21

Nordliches Derendorf Master Plan

Design 1992
Dusseldorf, Germany
City of Dusseldorf Planning Department
5,800,000 square feet

Our proposal recognizes the fact that we are living in an electronic era, which has replaced the mechanical one. In the movement from the era of utility to the era of information, electronic information systems become one of the new limitations to urban growth.

In Dusseldorf, one of these new limits is the system of radar and radio. The proximity of the airport's flight path causes certain height restrictions to be mapped onto this project. This mapping derives from the intersection of the radar and radio patterns, which produces an interference pattern that becomes the form-generator on the site.

1

2

3

4

5

6

7

8

9

10

11

12

13

14

Haus Immendorff

Design 1993
Dusseldorf, Germany
Professor Jorg Immendorff
13,300 square feet

This project for a cafe, private club, studio and office space for a painter is located on Dusseldorf's waterfront. The building's twisting form derives from an analysis of soliton waves which form non-linear interactions. Solitons undergo constant change and generate singular aqueous forms that alternately dissipate and regenerate as they move through the water. Haus Immendorff is composed of inner and outer volumes whose oblique surfaces intersect each other as they twist vertically, forming a vortex-like cone rising to the top of the building. The exterior volume is a stepped glass "skin" of bands of glass windows alternating with louvers set back at various widths from the glass. The inner volume is a solid wall with glazed cuts, to be used as a paint surface.

1

2

3

4

5

6

7

8

9

10

11

12

13

14

S C A L I N G S   T R A C I N G S

15

16

17

G R I D D I N G S

18

21

22

23

19

20

Firm Profile

Biographies

Peter Eisenman, FAIA

Peter Eisenman is an architect and educator. In 1980, after many years of teaching, writing, and producing respected theoretical work, he established his professional practice to focus exclusively on building. He has designed a wide range of prototypical projects including large-scale housing and urban design projects, innovative facilities for educational institutions, and a series of inventive private houses.

Among his built projects, the Wexner Center for the Visual Arts and Fine Arts Library at the Ohio State University in Columbus, completed in 1989, met with international acclaim, and received a 1993 National Honor Award from the American Institute of Architects. His project for social housing at Checkpoint Charlie at the Berlin Wall was honored by the West German Government, being featured on a postage stamp commemorating the 750th anniversary of the City of Berlin. He has built two office buildings in Tokyo: the Nunotani Corporation building, and the Koizumi Sangyo Corporation headquarters building, which received a 1991 National Honor Award from the American Institute of Architects.

In March 1993, opening ceremonies were held for the Greater Columbus Convention Center in Ohio, and construction had begun on the Aronoff Center for Design and Art at the University of Cincinnati. At present Peter Eisenman is working on the Center for the Arts at Emory University in Atlanta, Georgia; the master plan for Rebstockpark in Frankfurt, Germany; the high-rise Max Reinhardt Haus in Berlin; and an artist's cafe-studio in Dusseldorf.

In 1985, Peter Eisenman received a Stone Lion (First Prize) for his Romeo and Juliet Castles project at the Third International Architectural Biennale in Venice. He was one of two architects to represent the United States at the Fifth International Exhibition of Architecture of the Venice Biennale in 1991, and his projects are exhibited at museums and galleries around the world. Eisenman is the founder and former director of the Institute for Architecture and Urban Studies, an international think-tank for architectural criticism.

He has received numerous awards, including a Guggenheim Fellowship, the Brunner Award of the American Academy of Arts and Letters, and a grant from the National Endowment for the Arts.

His academic involvement has included teaching at Cambridge University, Princeton University, Yale University, and the Ohio State University. From 1982 to 1985 he was the Arthur Rotch Professor of Architecture at Harvard University, and in Fall 1993 he was the Eliot Noyes Visiting Design Critic at Harvard. Currently he is the first Irwin S. Chanin Distinguished Professor of Architecture at the Cooper Union in New York City.

Peter Eisenman is the author of several books, including *House X* (Rizzoli), *Fin d'Ou T HouS* (The Architectural Association), *Moving Arrows, Eros and Other Errors* (The Architectural Association), *Houses of Cards* (Oxford University Press) and *The Wexner Center for the Visual Arts* (Rizzoli). In addition, he was the editor of *Oppositions* journal and Oppositions Books, and he has published numerous essays and articles on his architectural theories in international magazines and journals.

Peter Eisenman received a Bachelor of Architecture degree from Cornell University, a Master of Architecture degree from Columbia University, MA and PhD degrees from the University of Cambridge, and an honorary Doctor of Fine Arts degree from the University of Illinois, Chicago.

George Kewin, AIA

George Kewin has recently led project teams for numerous international projects and competitions in Germany, including the Rebstockpark Master Plan, a five million square foot housing and commercial development in Frankfurt, Germany, which was the winning entry in an international competition in 1990. He was the Associate Principal-in-Charge for Eisenman Architects' entries in the Bahnhofsbereich Friedrichstrasse competition in Berlin, and the Nordliches Derendorf competition for a large-scale urban development in Dusseldorf. In addition, he was the Associate Principal-in-Charge for the Nunotani Office Building in Tokyo and the four-star Atocha 123 Hotel in Madrid. He is currently directing completion of comprehensive design and legal guidelines for the Rebstockpark Master Plan, and overseeing design development for a six-story cafe-bar and artists' studio space on the Dusseldorf Harbor in Germany.

Before joining Eisenman Architects in 1984, he was associated with Richard Meier and Partners, where he was project architect for the Des Moines Art Center Museum; and with the firm of Edward L. Barnes, where he was the project designer for the IBM Gallery of Art and Science and Equitable Tower in Manhattan.

George Kewin received his Master of Architecture degree from Harvard University, and his BA from the University of California at Berkeley. He has taught at the Graduate School of Architecture at the Ohio State University and served as a visiting critic at various other schools.

Richard N. Rosson, AIA

Richard Rosson is currently directing work on the Emory University Arts Center in Atlanta, Georgia, a $36 million, 126,000 square foot instructional and performance facility for the Department of Theater and Film Studies and the Department of Music. In addition, he is coordinating the work of Eisenman Architects' office on the Aronoff Center for Design and Art at the University of Cincinnati as the project enters the construction administration phase.

He was Project Manager for the fast-track design and construction of the $65 million, 530,000 square foot Convention Center in Columbus, Ohio, completed in March 1993, and also for a master plan of the Pittsburgh Technology Center, a 500,000 square foot laboratory and office park on the Monongahela River, for Carnegie Mellon University. He also oversaw the design of two buildings at the Center.

Since joining Eisenman Architects in 1985, he has been involved in various aspects of many projects, including the design and construction of a 350,000 square foot headquarters office building in Washington, DC and the renovation of the Harvard Club in New York City.

Formerly with Gresham Smith and Partners in Nashville, Richard Rosson served as Project Architect for hospitals and office buildings in the south-eastern United States and in Saudi Arabia.

Project Credits

House I
Architect: Peter Eisenman
Design Assistants: Russell Swanson,
Robinson O. Brown
Drawings: Russell Swanson,
Thomas Pritchard, Gregory A. Gale
Contractor: Bard Construction Co.

House II
Architect: Peter Eisenman
Design Assistants: Gregory A. Gale,
Robinson O. Brown
Drawings: Gregory A. Gale, Judith Turner,
Christopher Chimera
Structural Engineer: Geiger-Berger
Contractor: Dutton Smith

House III
Architect: Peter Eisenman
Structural Engineer: Geiger-Berger
Mechanical Engineer: George Langer
Contractor: Joseph Maloney

House IV
Architect: Peter Eisenman
Design Assistant: Rodney Knox
Drawings: Ellen Cheng Koutsoftas

House VI
Architect: Peter Eisenman
Design Assistants: Randall Korman,
Rodney Knox
Drawings: Read Furguson, Caroline Sidnam,
Wlliam Jackson
Model: Mark Mascheroni
Structural Engineer:
Robert Silman & Associates
Contractors: Arthur B. Deacon & Sons,
Robert Finney

House X
Architect: Peter Eisenman
Associate Architect: Leland Taliaferro
Assistants: Mark Cigolle, Livio Dimitriu, John
Nambu, Anthony Perrgola, Noel Quesada
Structural: Robert Silman Associates
(Ding Carbonell)
Mechanical: Arthur Spaet & Associates
(Arthur Fox)
Landscape: Nicholas Quennell
Cost: Stephen H. Falk
Model: Anthony Pergola
Axonometric Model: Sam Anderson
Photography: Dick Frank

Cannaregio Town Square
Architect: Peter Eisenman
Project Team: David Buege, John Nambu,
Joan Ockman
Models: Sam Anderson, Andrew Bartle
Model Photos: Dick Frank

House El even Odd
Architect: Peter Eisenman
Assistants: Mark Mascheroni,
Caroline Hancock, Tom Haworth
Collages: Walter Chatham, David Buege,
Cary Liu
Models: Tom Hut, John Leeper, Jim Uyeki,
John Regan
Coordinator: Eleanor Earle, Judy Geib
Structural Engineer: Robert Silman
Robert Silman Associates
Mechanical Engineer: Marvin Mass,
Cosentini Associates
Photography: Dick Frank

Madison Components Plant
Architect: Peter Eisenman

IBA Social Housing
Competition Phase
Architect: Eisenman/Robertson Architects
Partner-in-Charge: Peter Eisenman
Project Architects: Thomas Hut,
Thomas Leeser
Drawings: Michelle Andrew
Renderings: Brian Burr
Models: Sam Anderson, John Leeper,
Vera Marjanovic
Project Realization Phase
Architects: Eisenman/Robertson Architects;
Groetzebach, Plessow & Ehlers
Partners-in-Charge: Peter Eisenman,
Dietmar Groetzebach, Gunther Plessow
Associates-in-Charge: Thomas Leeser,
Wilfried Hartman
Project Team: Audrey Matlock, Doug Oliver,
Frank Chirico
Photos: Reinhard Goerner

Travelers Financial Center
Architect: Eisenman/Robertson Architects;
Trott & Bean Architects
Partners-in-Charge: Peter Eisenman,
Arthur Baker, Richard Trott
Associates-in-Charge: Richard Morris,
Faruk Yorganciouglu, Michael Burkey
Project Architects: Thomas Leeser,
Peter Thaler, Ross Woolley
Project Team: Andrea Brown, Wes Jones,
Mark Mascheroni, Joanne Rivkin,
Scott Sickeler
Structural Engineer: Office of Irwin Cantor
Mechanical Engineer: Cosentini Associates
General Contractor:
Turner Construction Company
Model Photographs: Dick Frank
Building Photographs:
Wolfgang Hoyt/ESTO

Firehouse for Engine Company 233
and Ladder Company 176
Architect: Eisenman/Robertson Architects
Partner-in-Charge: Peter Eisenman
SeniorArchitect: Arthur Baker

Project Architect: Ross Woolley
Project Team: David Winslow, Mark Wamble
Structural Engineer: Robert Silman
Mechanical Engineer: John Altieri
General Contractor: Bedell Associates

Fuller/Toms Loft
Architects: Peter Eisenman
& Faruk Yorgancioglu
Assistants: Richard & Candy Harder,
Glen Hamilton
Collaborators: Ragip Erdem, David Winslow,
James Brown
Engineering Consultants: John Altieri
Associates

Romeo and Juliet Castles
Architect: Eisenman/Robertson Architects
Partner-in-Charge: Peter Eisenman
Project Architects: Thomas Leeser,
Renato Rlzzi, Peter Thaler
Drawings: Raleigh Perkins, Susan Knauer,
Edward Carroll, Alexis Moser,
Carlene Ramus, Joseph Rosa
Graphics: Charles Crawford, James Brown,
Leslie Ryan
Models: Hiroshi Maruyama, Raleigh Perkins,
Christine Chang, Donna Cohen,
Guillaume Ehrman, Rajip Erdem,
Mara Graham, Kimberley Hoyt,
Marina Kieser, Jonathan Marvel,
Michel Mossessian, David Murphee,
Fabio Nonis, Peter Robson, Adam Silver,
Wolfgang Tschapeller, Charles Barclay,
Michael Casey
Model Photos: Dick Frank

Tokyo Opera House
Architects: Eisenman/Robertson Architects;
Richard Trott & Partners
Partners-in-Charge: Peter Eisenman,
Richard Trott
Project Architects: Thomas Leeser,
Hiroshi Maruyama, Benjamin Gianni
Project Team: Manou Ernster, David Goth,
Christian Kohl, Mark Schendal,
Joseph Tanney, Harvey Burns,
David Fratianne, Thomas Lanzelotti,
Kevin Miller, Sheri O'Reilly, David Mancino,
David Efaw, David Shultis, Kathleen Sullivan,
James Samuelson
Model Photographs: Dick Frank

Biocentrum
Architect: Eisenman Architects
Partner-in-Charge: Peter Eisenman
Associate-in-Charge: Thomas Leeser
Project Team: Hiroshi Maruyama,
David Biagi, Sylvain Boulanger, Ken Doyno,
Judy Geib, Holger Kleine, Christian Kohl,
Frederic Levrat, Greg Lynn, Carlene Ramus,
Wolfgang Rettenmaier, Madison Spencer,
Paul Sorum, Sarah Whiting, David Youse
Mechanical Engineer: Jaros, Baum & Bolles;

Augustine DiGiacomo
Structural Engineer:
Silman Associates, Robert Silman
Landscape Architect:
Hanna/Olin Ltd, Laurie Olin
Artist: Michael Heizer
Color Consultant: Robert Slutzky
Photography: Dick Frank Studios

La Villette
Architects: Eisenman/Robertson Architects;
Jacques Derrida, with Renato Rizzi
Architects-in-Charge: Peter Eisenman,
Jacques Derrida
Project Architects: Thomas Leeser,
Renato Rizzi
Project Team: Franco Alloca,
Paola Marzatico, Hiroshi Maruyama,
Manou Ernster
Model Photos: Dick Frank

University Art Museum
Architect: Eisenman/Robertson Architects
Partner-in-Charge: Peter Eisenman
Associate-in-Charge: Thomas Leeser
Project Architects: Hiroshi Maruyama,
Graeme Morland
Project Team: Michael Duncan,
Manou Ernster, Judy Geib, Fabio Ghersi,
Frances Hsu, Christian Kohl,
Paola Marzatico, Fabio Nonis, Joe Tanney,
Mark Wamble, Sarah Whiting, Gilly Youner
Gold Drawings: Mark Wamble
Landscape Architects:
Hanna/Olin, Philadelphia
Model Photos: Michael Moran

Progressive Corporation Office Building
Architects: Eisenman/Robertson Architects
Partner-in-Charge: Peter Eisenman
Associate-in-Charge: Thomas Leeser
Project Architects: Hiroshi Maruyama,
Fabio Nonis
Graphics and Exhibition Consultants:
Robert Slutzky
Model Photographs: Dick Frank

**Wexner Center for the Visual Arts
and Fine Arts Library**
Architect: Eisenman Architects;
Richard Trott & Partners Architects
Partners-in-Charge: Peter Eisenman,
Richard Trott
Directing Architects: George Kewin,
Michael Burdey
Project Architects: Arthur Baker,
Andrew Buchsbaum, Thomas Leeser,
Richard Morris, James Rudy,
Faruk Yorgancioglu
Project Team: Andrea Brown,
Edward Carroll, Robert Choeff, David Clark,
Chuck Crawford, Tim Decker,
Ellen Dunham, John Durschinger,

Frances Hsu, Wes Jones, Jim Linke,
Michael McInturf, Hiroshi Maruyama,
Mark Mascheroni, Alexis Moser, Harry Ours,
Joe Rosa, Scott Sickeler, Madison Spencer,
Mark Wamble
Landscape Architect:
Hanna Olin Ltd, Laurie Olin
Structural Engineer:
Lantz, Jones & Nebraska Inc., Tom Jones
Mechanical Engineer:
H.A. Williams & Associates
Lighting Design:
Jules Fisher & Paul Marantz Inc.
Civil Engineer: C.F. Bird & P.J. Bull Ltd
Security and Fire: Chapman & Ducibella Inc.
Graphics and Color: Robert Slutzky
Soils Engineer: Dunbar Geotechnical
Audio/Visual: Boyce Nemec
Acoustics: Jaffe Acoustics
Specifications: George Van Neil
Models: Scale Images, Albert Maloof,
Gene Servini
Renderings: Brian Burr
Model Photography: Dick Frank,
Wolfgang Hoyt
Construction Photographs: James Friedman,
Will Shively, D.G. Olshavsky/ARTOG
Final Photographs: Jeff Goldberg/ESTO,
D.G. Olshavsky/ARTOG
General Contractor: Dugan and Meyers,
Jim Smith, Project Manager
Mechanical Contractor: A.T.F. Mechanical
Inc., Bob Weiland, Project Manager
Electrical Contractor: Romanoff Electric,
Sib Goeiz, Project Superintendent
Plumbing Contractor: Radico Inc.,
Frank Czako, Project Manager
Steel Subcontractor: J.T. Edwards,
Jack Edwards, President

Carnegie Mellon Research Institute
Architect: Eisenman Architects
Principal-in-Charge: Peter Eisenman
Associate-in-Charge: Richard N. Rosson
Project Team: Lawrence Blough,
Kelly Hopkin, Richard Labonte, Greg Lynn,
Marisabel Marratt, Mark Wamble, Joe Walter
Project Assistants: Wendy Cox,
Simon Hubacher, Kim Tanzer,
Nicolas Vaucher, Sarah Whiting,
Katinka Zlonicky
Model Photographs: Dick Frank
Landscape Architect: Hanna/Olin Ltd,
Laurie Olin
Mechanical Engineer: Jaros, Baum & Bolles,
Augustine DiGiacomo
Structural Engineer: Ove Arup & Partners,
Guy Nordenson

Guardiola House
Architect: Eisenman Architects
Principal-in-Charge: Peter Eisenman
Associates-in-Charge: George Kewin,

Thomas Leeser
Project Architect: Antonio Sanmartin
Project Team: Nuno Mateus, Jan Kleihues,
Hiroshi Maruyama
Project Assistants:
Begona Fernandez Shaw, Felipe Guardiola,
Lise Anne Couture, Luis Rojo,
Michael McInturf, Madison Spencer,
Simon Hubacher, Maximo Victoria,
Frederic Levrat, Anne Marx, Robert Choeff,
Julie Shurtz, Dagmar Schimkus
Structural Engineer: Gerardo Rodriguez
Photography: Dick Frank

Aronoff Center for Design and Art
Architect: Eisenman Architects;
Lorenz & Williams Inc.
Principal-in-Charge: Peter Eisenman,
Richard Roediger
Associates-in-Charge: George Kewin,
Richard Rosson, Jerome Flynn
Project Architects: Donna Barry, Greg Lynn,
Michael McInturf, Joseph Walter
Project Team: Lawrence Blough,
Kelly Hopkin, Edward Mitchell,
Astrid Perlbinder, Brad Winkeljohn (EA),
Joseph Mitlo, Shari Rotella, Jerome Scott,
James Schriefer, Michael Schuyler (LWI)
Project Assistants: Vincent Costa,
Reid Freeman, Nazli Gonensay,
Martin Houston, Richard Labonte,
Corrine Nacinovic, Jean-Gabriel Neukomn,
Karen Pollock, Joe Schott, Jim Wilson,
Jason Winstanley, Leslie Young (EA)
Construction Manager: Dugan & Meyers Inc,
Francis Dugan, Daniel Dugan,
Andy Englehart, Steve Klinder
Civil Engineer: United Consultants
Landscape Architect: Hargreaves Associates
Engineering: Lorenz & Williams Inc.
Acoustical Design: Jaffe Acoustics
Lighting Design: Fisher Marantz
Audiovisual Design: Boyce Nemec Designs
Color Consultant: Donald Kaufman Color
Photography: Dick Frank

Koizumi Sangyo Office Building
Architects: Eisenman Architects;
K Architects and Associates, Tokyo
Partners-in-Charge: Peter Eisenman,
Kojiro Kitayama
Associate-in-Charge: George Kewin
Project Architects: Hiroshi Maruyama (EA),
Minoru Fujii (KA)
Project Team: Lawrence Blough,
Robert Choeff, Lise Anne Couture,
Begona Fernandez Shaw, Frederic Levrat,
Dagmar Schimkus, Julie Shurtz,
Mark Wamble (EA), Itaru Miyakawa,
Tamihiro Motozawa, Hiroyuki Kubodera,
Kazuhiro Isimaru, Susumu Arasaki,
Yujiro Yamasaki (KA)

Siena Bank Master Plan
Architects: Eisenman Architects;
with Renat Rizzi
Project Architect: Thomas Leeser
Photographer: Dick Frank Studi

Greater Columbus Convention Center
Architects: Eisenman Architects;
Richard Trott and Partners Architects Inc.
Principals-in-Charge: Peter Eisenman,
Richard Trott, Jean Gordon
Associates-in-Charge: Richard Rosson,
Michael Burkey
Project Managers: Tracy Aronoff,
Philip Babb, Thomas Ingledue, Jerome Scott
Project Architects: Mark Wamble,
Thomas Leeser
Project Team: Madison Spenser,
Richard Labonte, Kathleen Meyer,
Dean Maltz, David Trautman,
Lewis Jacobsen, Joe Walter, Nuno Mateus
(EA); Jerry Kehlmeier, David Goth,
Lu Schubert, Kristina Ennis, Tim Decker,
John Meegan, Dave Reltenwald,
Blaide Lewis, James Dean, George Van Neil,
Carol Hummel, Chun Shin, Karen McCoy,
Al Brook (RTPA)
Project Assistants: Yvhang Kong,
John Durschinger, John Curran,
Chiara Scortecci, Ilkka Tarkkanen, Jon Malis,
Andres Viditz-Ward, Giovanni Rivolta,
Francesca Acerboni, Jason Winstanley,
John Juryj, Daniel Perez,
Andres Blanco (EA)
Engineers: Lorenz & Williams Inc.
Principal-in Charge: Richard Roediger
Project Managers: Timothy McCrate
(Structural), John Putnam (Mechanical),
Jack Kolb (Mechanical), Timothy Raberding
(Electrical), Thomas Fischer (Construction
Administration)
Civil Engineer: Moody/Nolan Ltd,
Howard Nolan
Code Consultant: Oregon Group Architects,
Jane Voisard
Roofing: Simpson, Gumperts & Heger Inc,
Kevin Cash
Graphic Design: Mayer/Reed, Michael Reed
Lighting: Jules Fisher & Paul Marantz Inc,
Richard Renfro
Acoustics: Jaffe Acoustics Inc., Mark Holden
Construction Manager:
Turner/Smoot/Zunt, Joel Sloan,
Project Manager
Photography: Dick Frank Studio,
ARTOG/D.G. Olshavsky,
Jeff Goldberg/ESTO

Banyoles Olympic Hotel
Architect: Eisenman Architects
Principal-in-Charge: Peter Eisenman
Associate-in-Charge: George Kewin
Project Designers: Begona Fernandez-Shaw,
Nuno Mateus

Project Team: Ed Mitchell, Anne Peters,
Weiland Vajen
Project Assistants: Lawrence Blough,
John Durschinger, Kelly Hopkin,
Martin Houston, Yuhang Kong,
Richard Labonte, Mari Marratt,
Tom Popoff, Henry Urbach, Joe Walter,
Mark Wamble, Leslie Young
Structural Engineer:
"Static" Ingenieria De Construccion,
Gerardo Rodriguez
Model Photographs: Dick Frank

Cooper Union Housing
Architects: Eisenman Architects;
Thomas Leeser
Principal-in-Charge: Peter Eisenman
Associate-in-Charge: George Kewin
Project Designer: Nuno Mateus
Project Team: Ed Mitchell, Joe Walter,
John Durschinger, Yuhang Kong,
Tom Popoff, Wieland Vajen
Project Assistants: Andreas Blanco,
Lawrence Blough, Reid Freeman,
Begona Fernandez-Shaw, Kelly Hopkin,
Jake Malis, Mari Marratt, Tony Pergola,
Astrid Perlbinder, Anne Peters,
Inigo Rodriguez-San Pedro, Leslie Smith,
Madison Spencer, Ilkka Tarkkanen,
Mark Wamble, Jim Wilson
Structural Consultants:
Severud Associates Consulting Engineers
PC Mechanical, Plumbing, Electrical
Consultants: Jaros, Baum & Bolles
Consulting Engineers
Zoning Consultant: Michael Parley
Code Consultant: Super Structures
Model Photography: Dick Frank

Groningen Music-Video Pavilion
Architect: Eisenman Architects
Principal-in-Charge: Peter Eisenman
Associate-in-Charge: George Kewin
Project Architect: Jorg Gleiter
Project Team: Andrea Stipa,
Anton Viditz-Ward, Reid Freeman

Nunotani Office Building
Architect: Eisenman Architects
Principal-in-Charge: Peter Eisenman
Associate-in-Charge: George Kewin
Project Architects: Mark Wamble,
Tracy Aronoff
Project Team: David Trautman, John Curran
Project Assistants: Thor Thors,
Hans-Georg Berndsen, Karen Pollock,
David Johnson, Evan Yassy,
Gregory Merryweather, Andrea Stipa,
Jason Winstanley, Andre Kikoski
Construction Manager and Contractor:
The Zenitaka Corporation;
Yoshimichi Hama, Director Manager,
Yoshiteru Kagikawa, Director,
Keiichi Kuwana, Deputy Manager

Model Photography: Dick Frank Studio
Building Photography:
Shigeo Ogawa/Shinkenchiku

Atocha 123 Hotel
Architects: Eisenman Architects;
The Austin Company, SA
Principals-in-Charge: Peter Eisenman,
F.E. "Brownie" Higgs
Associate-in-Charge: George Kewin
Project Managers: David Koons,
Jesus Salgado Marques, Luis Guerrero
Project Architects: Gregory Luhan,
Jorg Gleiter, John Curran, Nuno Mateus,
Mark Searls (EA), Antonio de la Morena,
M. Magdalena Velez,
Ramon Jose Farinas (AC)
Project Team: Tracy Aronoff, Mary Marratt,
Andrea Stipa, Joe Walter, Jason Winstanley,
Donald Skinner, John Maze, Tom Gilman,
Andrew Burmeister
Project Assistants: Donna Barry,
Rosa-Maria Colina, Brooks Critchfield,
Angelo Directo, Winka Dubbledam,
John Durschinger, Martin Felsen,
Brad Gildea, Christophe Guinard,
Jan Hinrichs, Brad Khouri, Andre Kikoski,
Robert Kim, Justin Korhammer,
Alexander Levi, Luc Leveque,
Frederic Levrat, James McCrery,
Gregory Merryweather, David Moore,
Maureen Murphy-Ochsner, Karim Musfy,
Alex Nussbaumer, Karen Pollock,
Stefania Rinaldi, Raquel Sendra,
Jody Sheldon, Marc Stotzer,
Masahiro Suzuki, David Swanson,
Thor Thors
Structural Engineer: The Austin Company,
SA, Fernando De La Frost,
Fernando Yandela Terrosa
Contractor: The Austin Company SA
Photography: Dick Frank

Rebstockpark Master Plan
Architect: Eisenman Architects
Consulting Architect:
Albert Speer & Partner GmbH
Landscape Architect: Hanna/Olin Ltd
Consulting Landscape Architect:
Boedeker, Wagenfeld, Niemeyer & Partners
Traffic Planning:
Durth Roos Consulting GmbH
Principals-in-Charge: Peter Eisenman,
Albert Speer, Laurie Olin
Associates-in-Charge:
George Kewin, Gerhard Brand
Project Managers: Norbert Holthausen,
Michael Denkel, Shirley Kressel,
Karina Aicher
Project Architects: Joachim Bothe,
Jorg Gleiter, Nuno Mateus, Mark Wamble,
Matthew White
Project Team: Pornchai Boonsom,
Brad Gildea, Judith Haase,

Justin Korhammer, Luc Levesque,
Gregory Merryweather, Steven Meyer,
Karim Musfy, Andrea Stipa, Marc Stotzer,
Jason Winstanley, Corinna Wydler
Project Assistants: Donna Barry,
Rosa-Maria Colina, John Curran,
John Durschinger, Michael Eastwood,
Carolina Garcia, Nazli Gononsay,
John Juryj, Andre Kikoski, Stephano Libardi,
Greg Lynn, James McCrery, Edward Mitchell,
Jean Nukomn, Karen Pollock, Jon Stephens
Models: Eisenman Architects
Photography: Dick Frank Studios

Alteka Office Building
Architect: Eisenman Architects
Principal-in-Charge: Peter Eisenman
Associate-in-Charge: Richard Rosson
Project Architect: Mark Wamble
Project Team: Gregory Merryweather,
Nazli Gononsay
Project Assistants: Mina Mei-Szu Chow,
Rosa-Maria Colina, Cornelius Deckert,
Robert Kim, Maria Laurent, Frederic Levrat,
Pierre-Olivier Milanini, Hadrian Predock,
Jason Winstanley
Photography: Dick Frank

Emory Center for the Arts
Architect: Eisenman Architects
Principal-in-Charge: Peter Eisenman
Associate-in-Charge: Richard Rosson
Project Manager: Tracy Aronoff
Project Architects: Selim Koder,
Frederic Levrat, Mark Searls
Project Team: Philip Babb,
James Gettinger, Brad Gildea,
Timothy Hyde, Richard Labonte, Ingel Liou,
Gregory Luhan, James Luhur,
James McCrery, Maureen Murphy-Ochsner,
Lindy Roy, David Schatzle, Joseph Walter
Project Assistants: Ted Arleo, Donna Barry,
Federico Beulcke, Sergio Bregante,
Marc Breitler, Winka Dubbeldam,
Daniel Dubowitz, John Durschinger,
David Eisenmann, Abigail Feinerman,
Ralf Feldmeier, Martin Felsen,
Sigrid Geerlings, Robert Holton,
Keelan Kaiser, Patrick Keane, James Keen,
Brad Khouri, Rolando Kraeher, Joseph Lau,
Maria Laurent, Vincent LeFeuvre,
Claudine Lutolf, John Maze, Mark McCarthy,
Steven Meyer, Julien Monfort, David Moore,
Yayoi Ogo, Debbie Park, Axel Rauenbusch,
Ali Reza Razavi, Mirko Reinecke, Tilo Ries,
Stefania Rinaldi, David Ruzicka, Setu Shah,
Tod Slaboden, Giovanni Soleti,
Lucas Steiner, Helene Van gen Hassend,
Marcus Wallner, Benjamin Wayne,
Lois Weinthal, Erin Vali, Irina Verona
Landscape Architect: Hanna/Olin Ltd,
Laurie Olin, Chris Allen, Cora Olgyay
Structural Engineer:
Stanley D. Lindsey & Associates Inc.,

Stanley Lindsey, Tommy Hagood
Mechanical & Electrical Engineer:
Nottingham, Brook & Pennington Inc.,
Charles Pennington, Neil Wych
Acoustical Consultant:
Kirkegaard & Associates Inc.,
Larry Kirkegaard, David Eplee, Brian Cline
Theater and Lighting Design: Theatre
Projects Consultants Inc., Richard Pilbrow,
Robert Long, Peter Lucking, Ben Boltin
Cost Analysis: Donnell Consultants Inc.,
Stewart Donnell, Athol Joffe
Photography: Dick Frank

Max Reinhardt Haus
Architect: Eisenman Architects
Principal-in-Charge: Peter Eisenman
Associate-in-Charge: George Kewin
Project Architects: Edward Mitchell,
Lindy Roy, Richard Labonte
Project Team: Armand Biglari, Brad Gildea,
Norbert Holthausen, Gregory Luhan,
Stefania Rinaldi, David Schatzle,
Jon Stephens
Project Assistants: Federico Beulske,
Mark Bretler, Andrew Burmeister,
Robert Holten, Patrick Keane, Brad Khouri,
Joseph Lau, Vincent LeFeuvre,
Fabian Lemmel, John Maze, Steven Meyer,
Debbie Park, Silke Potting, Benjamin Wade
Landscape Architect: Hanna/Olin Ltd,
Laurie Olin, Shirley Kressel,
Matthew W. White
Color Consultant: Donald Kaufman Color
Structural Engineer: Severud Associates,
Edward M. Messina, Edward DiPaolo
Mechanical Engineer: Jaros, Baum & Bolles,
Augustine A. DiGiacomo,
Kenneth J. Zuar
Wind & Shadow Studies: Spacetec
Datengewinnung, Freiburg, Germany
Cost Estimating: Donnell Consultants Inc.,
Stewart Donnell
Computer Images: Edward Keller
Photography: Dick Frank

Nordliches Derendorf Master Plan
Urban Designers: Eisenman Architects;
Hanna/Olin Landscape Architects
Principals-in-Charge: Peter Eisenman,
Laurie Olin
Associates-in-Charge: George Kewin,
Shirley Kressel
Project Architects: Winka Dubbledam,
Norbert Holthausen, Donna Barry,
Matthew White
Project Team: Edgar Cozzio,
James Gettinger, Brad Gildea, Jorg Lesser,
Jon Stephens, James McCrery
Project Assistants: Barbera Aderbeauer,
Armand Biglari, Frederico Buelcke,
Andy Burmeister, John Durschinger,
Martin Felsen, Patrick Keane, Brad Khouri,
Selim Koder, Fabian Lemmel,

Frederic Levrat, Gregory Luhan,
Maureen Murphy-Ochsner, Stephania
Rinaldi, Lindy Roy, David Schatzle (EA),
Bobbie Huffman, David Rubin,
Howard Supnik, Karen Skafte (HO)
Traffic Planning: Durth Roos Consulting,
Hans-Joachim Fischer
Color Consultants: Donald Kaufman Color,
Donald Kaufman, Taffy Dahl
Computer Modeling: Mathematica Program,
Seamus Moran, Physicist
Photography: Dick Frank, Brian Connelly

Haus Immendorff
Architect: Eisenman Architects
Principal-in-Charge: Peter Eisenman
Associate-in-Charge: George Kewin
Project Architect: Lindy Roy
Project Team: David Schatzle,
Patrick Keane, James Luhur
Project Assistants: Barbara Adabauer,
Ted Arleo, Marc Bretler,
Andrew Burmeister, Chi Yi Chang,
Winka Dubbeldam, David Eisenmann,
Abigail Feinerman, Annette Kahler,
Fabian Lemmel, Jung Kue Liou,
Gregory Luhan, Max Muller,
Mirko Reinecke, Tilo Ries, Lucas Steiner
Construction Manager:
Phillip Holzmann HOG
Structural Engineer:
Severud Associates Consulting Engineers,
PC Mechanical, Plumbing, Electrical
Engineer: Jaros, Baum & Bolles
Photography: Dick Frank

Associates & Collaborators

Francesca Acerboni
Barbara Aderbeauer
Franco Alloca
Tobias Amme
Sam Anderson
Michelle Andrew
Lise Anne Couture
Ted Arleo
Tracy Aronoff, AIA
Phillip Babb, AIA
Arthur Baker
Charles Barclay
Donna Barry
Andrew Bartle
David Beers
Hans-Georg Berndsen
Federico Beulcke
David Biagi
Herve Biele
Armand Biglari
Andres Blanco
Lawrence Blough
Pornchai Boonsom
Joachim Bothe
Sylvain Boulanger
Sergio Bregante
Marc Bretler
Sam Britton
Andrea Brown
James Brown
Andrew Buchsbaum
David Buege
Frederico Buelcke
Andrew Burmeister
Harvey Burns
Francine Cadogan
Edward Carroll
Michael Casey
Ronald Castellano
Christine Chang
Chi-Yi Chang
Frank Chirico
Robert Choeff
David Clark
Donna Cohen
Rosa-Maria Colina
Catherine Colla
Sarah Connoly
Vincent Costa
Wendy Cox
Edgar Cozzio
Charles Crawford
Nestor Crubellati
John Curran

Christophe Dahm
Cynthia Davidson
Ken Doyno
Winka Dubbeldam
Daniel Dubowitz
Michael Duncan
Ellen Dunham
John Durschinger
Arthur Dyess
Michael Eastwood
David Efaw
Guillaume Ehrman
Peter Eisenman, FAIA
David Eisenmann
Rajip Erdem
Manou Ernster
Abigail Feinerman
Ralf Feldmeier
Simon Fellmeth
Martin Felsen
Begona Fernandez-Shaw
Scott Ferris
David Fratianne
Reid Freeman
Jason Frontera
Carolina Garcia
Sigrid Geerlings
Judy Geib
James Gettinger
Fabio Ghersi
Benjamin Gianni
Brad Gildea
Jorg Gleiter
Nazli Gononsay
Mercedes Gonzalez
David Goth
Mara Graham
Susanne Grau
Stephen Griek
Felipe Guardiola
Judith Haase
Daniel Hale
Jan Hartman
Robert Holten
Norbert Holthausen
Robert Holton
Kelly Hopkin
Martin Houston
Kimberley Hoyt
Frances Hsu
Simon Hubacher
Joanne Humphries
Thomas Hut
Timothy Hyde
Diana Ibrahim

Antoinette Jackson
Lewis Jacobsen
Mary Jane McRory
David Johnson
Wes Jones
Jan Jurgens
John Juryj
Annette Kahler
Keelan Kaiser
Rudolph Kammeri
Patrick Keane
James Keen
May Kellner
Therese Kelly
George Kewin
Brad Khouri
Marina Kieser
Andre Kikoski
Rebecca Klapper
Jan Kleihues
Holger Kleine
Susan Knauer
Selim Koder
Christian Kohl
Yvhang Kong
David Koons
Erin Korff
Justin Korhammer
Rolando Kraeher
Kenneth Kraus
Miroslaw Krawczynski
Jung Kue Liou
Richard Labonte
Thomas Lanzelotti
Bernadette Latour
Joseph Lau
Maria Laurent
Vincent Le-Feuvre
Joseph Lechowicz
John Leeper
Jorg Leeser
Thomas Leeser
Fabian Lemmel
Luc Levesque
Frederic Levrat
Andrew Liang
Stephano Libardi
Alexandra Ligotti
Jim Linke
Ingel Liou
Gregory Luhan
James Luhur
Claudine Lutolf
Greg Lynn

236

Jake Malis
Dean Maltz
David Mancino
Vera Marjanovic
Marisabel Marratt
Hiroshi Maruyama
Jonathan Marvel
Anne Marx
Paola Marzatico
Mark Mascheroni
Nuno Mateus
Audrey Matlock
Dominik Mayer
John Maze
Mark McCarthy
James McCrery
Meegan McFarland
Michael Mcinturf
Gregory Merryweather
Will Meyer
Kathleen Meyer
Steven Meyer
Kevin Miller
Benedicte Mioli
Edward Mitchell
Julian Monfort
David Moore
Graeme Morland
Richard Morris
Alexis Moser
Michel Mossessian
Matthias Muffert
Max Muller
David Murphee
Maureen Murphy-Ochsner
Karim Musfy
Corrine Nacinovic
John Nambu
Jean-Gabriel Neukomn
Fabio Nonis
Jean Nukomn
Alex Nussbaumer
Patrick O'Brien
Sheri O'Oreilly
Joan Ockman
Yayoi Ogo
Doug Oliver
Elizabeth Pacot
Katherina Panagiotou
Debbie Park
Daniel Perez
Tony Pergola
Raleigh Perkins
Astrid Perlbinder
John Peter-Hartman

Anne Peters
Angela Phillips
Karen Pollock
Tom Popoff
Silke Potting
Carlene Ramus
Axel Rauenbusch
Rachel Ravitz
Jurgen Reimann
Mirko Reinecke
Mirko Reinecke
Wolfgang Rettenmaier
Ali Reza Razavi
Tilo Ries
Stefania Rinaldi
Giovanni Rivolta
Miranda Robbins
Peter Robson
Inigo Rodriguez San Pedro
Luis Rofriguez
Christian Rogner
Luis Rojo
Louise Rosa
Joseph Rosa
Richard Rosson, AIA
Lindy Roy
David Ruzicka
Leslie Ryan
James Samuelson
Antonio Sanmartin
Mario Santin
David Schatzle
Mark Schendal
Florian Scheytt
Dagmar Schimkus
Michael Schmidt
Joe SchoK
Chiara Scortecci
Jerome Scott
Mark Searls, AIA
Raquel Sendra
John Seppanen
Setu Shah
Jody Sheldon
Tadao Shimitzu
David Shultis
Julie Shurtz
Scott Sickeler
Stefen Siebrecht
Adam Silver
Tod Slaboden
Leslie Smith
Jeff Smith
Barry Smyth
Giovanni Soleti

Angelika Solleder
Paul Sorum
Lucy Sosa
Michael Speaks
Madison Spencer
Lucas Steiner
Jon Stephens
Andrea Stipa
Marc Stotzer
Kathleen Sullivan
Masahiro Suzuki
David Swanson
Joseph Tanney
Kim Tanzer
likka Tarkkanen
Peter Thaler
Sabine Thiel
Thor Thors
Lisa Toms
David Trautman
Wolfgang Tschapeller
Henry Urbach
Weiland Vajen
Erin Vali
Helena Van gen Hassend
Nicholas Vaucher
Irina Verona
Maximo Victoria
Andres Viditz-Ward
Benjamin Wade
Marcus Wallner
Joseph Walter
Mark Wamble
Janine Washington
Benjamin Wayne
Lois Weinthal
Matthew White
Sarah Whiting
Alexander Wiedemann
Jim Wilson.
Brad Winkeljohn
Jason Winstanley
Marcus Witta
Colby Wong
Corinna Wydler
Evan Yassy
Chi Yi Chang
Faruk Yorgancioglu
Gilly Youner
Leslie Young
David Youse
Harry Zernike
Katinka Zlonicky

Chronological List of Buildings & Projects

*Indicates work featured in this book
(see Selected and Current Works).

Liverpool Cathedral Competition
1960
Liverpool, England

Boston City Hall Competition
1961
Boston, Massachusetts
(with Anthony Eardley)

Boston Architectural Center Competition
1963
Boston, Massachusetts
(with Michael Graves)

**The American Institute of Architects
Headquarters Competition**
1964
Washington, DC
(with Michael Graves)

**Jersey Corridor Project: A Case Study of a
Linear City in the Jersey Corridor between
New York and Philadelphia**
1964–1966
(with Anthony Eardley and Michael
Graves)

Arts Center Competition
1965
University of California
(with Michael Graves)

Manhattan Waterfront Project
1966
New York, New York
Museum of Modern Art
(with Michael Graves)

***House I**
1967–1968
Princeton, New Jersey
Mr and Mrs Bernard M. Barenholz

Townhouse Project
1968
Princeton, New Jersey

***House II**
1969–1970
Hardwick, Vermont
Mr and Mrs Richard Falk

***House III**
1969–1971
Lakeville, Connecticut
Mr and Mrs Robert Miller

***House IV**
1971
Falls Village, Connecticut

House V
1972

***House VI**
1972–1975
Cornwall, Connecticut
Mr and Mrs Richard Frank

Low-Rise High-Density Housing
1973
Staten Island, New York
New York State Urban Development
Corporation

House VIII
1973

***House X**
1975
Bloomfield Hills, Michigan
Mr and Mrs Arnold Aronoff

House 11a
1978
Palo Alto, California
Mr and Mrs Forster

***Cannaregio Town Square**
1978
Venice, Italy
Municipal Government of Venice

***House El even Odd**
1980

Eisenman Robertson Architects

Pioneer Courthouse Square Competition
1980
Portland, Oregon

***Madison Components Plant**
1981–1982
Madison, Indiana
Cummins Engine Company

New Brunswick Theological Seminary
1981–1982
New Brunswick, New Jersey
New Brunswick Theological Seminary

***IBA Social Housing**
1981–1985
Berlin, West Germany
Hauert Noack, GmbH & Company

Beverly Hills Civic Center
1982
Beverly Hills, California

***Travelers Financial Center**
1983–1986
Hempstead, New York
Fair Oaks Development and Schottenstein
Properties (with Trott & Bean Architects,
Columbus, Ohio)

***Firehouse for Engine Company 233 and
Ladder Company 176**
1983–1985
Brooklyn, New York
City of New York

***Wexner Center for the Visual Arts
and Fine Arts Library**
1983–1989
Columbus, Ohio
Ohio State University

Fin d'Ou T Hou S
1983

*Romeo and Juliet Castles
1985
Verona, Italy

*Tokyo Opera House
1985
Tokyo, Japan
City of Tokyo

Cite Unseen 11
1985
Milan, Italy
XV Triennale di Milano

Hardware
1986
Franz Schneider Brakel GmbH & Co.

House
1986
Palm Beach, Florida
Mr Leslie Wexner

Jewlery
1986
Cleto Munari

*University Art Museum
1986
Long Beach, California
California State University at Long Beach

*Progressive Corporation Office Building
1986
Cleveland, Ohio
Progressive Corporation

Museum of Futurism
1986
Rovereto, Italy

Eisenman Architects

Tableware
1986
Swid Powell

*Biocentrum
1987
Frankfurt am Main, West Germany
J.W. Goethe University

EuroDisney Hotel
1987
Paris, France
Disney Development Company

*Fuller/Toms Loft
1987
New York, New York
Ms Fuller/Mr Toms

*La Villette
1987
Paris, France
Establissement Public du Parc de la Vilette

*Carnegie Mellon Research Institute
1987–1989
Pittsburgh, Pennsylvania
Carnegie Mellon University

*Guardiola House
1988
Cadiz, Spain
D. Javier Guardiola

*Aronoff Center for Design and Art
1988–present
Cincinnati, Ohio
University of Cincinnati

*Koizumi Sangyo Office Building
1988–1990
Tokyo, Japan
Koizumi Sangyo Corporation

*Siena Bank Master Plan
1988
Siena, Italy
Siena Chamber of Commerce

*Greater Columbus Convention Center
1989–1993
Columbus, Ohio
Greater Columbus Convention Center
Authority

*Banyoles Olympic Hotel
1989
Banyoles, Spain
Consorci Pel Desenvolupament De La Vila
Olimpica

*Cooper Union Student Housing
1989
New York, New York
The Cooper Union

Zoetermeer Houses
1989
The Netherlands
Geerlings Vastgoed B.V., J.G.A. Geerlings

*Groningen Music-Video Pavilion
1990
Groningen, The Netherlands
Groningen City Festival

*Nunotani Office Building
1990–1992
Tokyo, Japan
Nunotani Corporation

*Atocha 123 Hotel
1990–1993
Madrid, Spain
Sociedad Belga de Los Pinares De el Paular

Knoll Textiles
1990
The Knoll Group

*Rebstockpark Master Plan
1990–present
Frankfurt, Germany
City of Frankfurt, Dieter Bock and
Buropark an der Frankfurter Messe GdR

*Alteka Office Building
1991
Tokyo, Japan
Alteka Corporation

*Emory Center for the Arts
1991
Atlanta, Georgia
Emory University

Advanta Haus
1992
Berlin, Germany
Advanta Management AG, Dieter Bock

*Max Reinhardt Haus
1992
Berlin, Germany
Advanta Management AG, Dieter Bock
Ostinvest, Klaus-Peter Junge and Klaus
Dieter

*Nordliches Derendorf Master Plan
1992
Dusseldorf, Germany
City of Dusseldorf Planning Department

Zurich Insurance Headquarters Study
1992
Frankfurt, Germany
Buropark an der Frankfurter Messe

Friedrichstrasse Competition
1992–1993
Berlin, Germany
Advanta Management AG and Ostinvest

*Haus Immendorff
1993
Dusseldorf, Germany
Professor Jorg Immendorff

Madgeburg, Damaschkeplatz II
1993
Madgeburg, Germany
Hauert and Noack GmbH & Co.

Cities of Artificial Excavation
1993–1994
Montreal, Canada
Canadian Centre for Architecture

**Tours Regional Music Conservatory and
Contemporary Arts Center Competition**
1993–1994
Tours, France
City of Tours
(with Jean Yves Barrier Architect)

Architecture of Display
1995
New York, New York
Comme des Garçons, The Architectural
League

Celebration Fire Station
1995
Orlando, Florida
Disney Development Company

United Nations Headquarters
1995
Geneva, Switzerland

Awards & Exhibitions

*Indicates catalog

Awards

Architectural Design Citation
Progressive Architecture
Center for the Arts
Emory University, Atlanta, Georgia
1993

Architectural Projects Honor Award
New York Chapter, American Institute
of Architects
Center for the Arts
Emory University, Atlanta, Georgia
1993

Citation
New York Chapter, American Institute
of Architects
Nunotani Office Building
Nunotani Corporation, Tokyo, Japan
1993

National Honor Award
American Institute of Architects
Wexner Center for the Visual Arts
and Fine Arts Library
Ohio State University, Columbus, Ohio
1993

Architectural Design Award
Progressive Architecture
Alteka Office Building
Tokyo, Japan
1992

Architectural Design Award
Progressive Architecture
College of Design, Architecture,
Art and Planning
University of Cincinnati, Cincinnati, Ohio
1991

**Fifth International Exhibition of
Architecture of the Venice Biennale**
College of Design, Architecture,
Art and Planning
University of Cincinnati, Cincinnati, Ohio
1991

First Prize
Invited International Competition
Rebstockpark Master Plan
Frankfurt, Germany
1991

National Honor Award
American Institute of Architects
Koizumi Sangyo Building
Koizumi Sangyo Corporation
Tokyo, Japan
1991

Architectural Design Award
Progressive Architecture
Banyoles Olympic Hotel
Banyoles, Spain
1990

Architectural Design Citation
Progressive Architecture
Carnegie Mellon Research Institute
Carnegie Mellon University
Pittsburgh, Pennsylvania
1990

Architectural Design Citation
Progressive Architecture
Guardiola House, Cadiz, Spain
1989

Architectural Projects Honor Award
New York Chapter, American Institute
of Architects
Carnegie Mellon Research Institute
Carnegie Mellon University
Pittsburgh, Pennsylvania
1989

Architectural Projects Honor Award
New York Chapter, American Institute
of Architects
Guardiola House, Cadiz, Spain
1989

First Prize
Invited International Competition
Banyoles Olympic Hotel
Banyoles, Spain
1989

First Prize
Invited International Competition
Greater Columbus Convention Center
Columbus, Ohio
1989

Gold Medal
Fifth World Biennial of Architecture
Interarch
Houses of Cards
1989

Interior Project Citation
New York Chapter, American Institute
of Architects
Fuller/Toms Loft
New York, New York
1989

National Honor Award
American Institute of Architects
IBA Social Housing
Berlin, Germany
1988

Architectural Design Citation
Progressive Architecture
University Art Museum
University of California at Long Beach
Long Beach, California
1987

Special Prize
Invited International Competition
Biocentrum
Frankfurt, West Germany
1987

Architectural Design Award
Progressive Architecture
Wexner Center for the Visual Arts and
Fine Arts Library
Ohio State University, Columbus, Ohio
1985

Award for Excellence in Design
New York City Art Commission
Firehouse for Engine 233 & Ladder
Company 176
New York, New York
1985

Stone Lion
Third International Architectural
Biennale
Romeo and Juliet Castles
1985

First Prize
Invited International Competition
Wexner Center for the Visual Arts and
Fine Arts Library
Ohio State University, Columbus, Ohio
1983

Special First Prize
West Berlin Invited International
Competition
South Friedrichstadt
West Berlin, West Germany
1981

Architectural Design Citation
Progressive Architecture
House 11a
1979

Architectural Design Citation
Progressive Architecture
House X
1976

Exhibitions

Cities of Artificial Excavation:
The Work of Peter Eisenman, 1978–1988
Madrid, Spain
March, 1995

*Cities of Artificial Excavation:
The Work of Peter Eisenman, 1978–1988
Centre Canadien d'Architecture
Montreal
March–June 1994

*Color of an Artist: Haus Immendorff
Galerie fur Architektur Renate Kammer
und Angelika Hinrichs
Hamburg, Germany
December 1993–January 1994

M Emory Games
Harvard University Graduate School of
Design
Cambridge, Massachusetts
December 1993–January 1994

GA International 93:
Center for the Arts, Emory University
GA Gallery
Tokyo, Japan
April–May 1993
K2 Gallery
Osaka, Japan
May–June 1993

*Griddings, Scalings, Tracings and
Foldings in the Work of Peter Eisenman
Museu de Arte de Sao Paulo
Sao Paulo, Brazil
May–June, 1993

Peter Eisenman: Why Pink?
Sadock & Uzzan Galerie
Paris, France
March–June 1993

*Museo d'arte e architettura
Museo Cantonale d'Arte
Lugano, Switzerland
September–November 1992

The Frankfurt Rebstockpark Project
Finanzbehorde Eingang Gansemarkt
Hamburg, Germany
July 1992
*Hamburgurgische Architektenkammer
Hamburg, Germany
June 1992
*Deutsches Architekturmuseum
Frankfurt, Germany
December 1992–January 1993

*Fifth International Exhibition of
Architecture at the 1991 Venice Biennale
The Contemporary Arts Center
Cincinnati, Ohio
April–May 1992
The Riffe Gallery
Columbus, Ohio
June–August 1992
The Cleveland Center for
Contemporary Art
Cleveland, Ohio
September–November 1992
Dayton Art Institute
Dayton, Ohio
December 1992–January 1993

*Architecture Triennale for The World
Architecture Exposition
Nara, Japan
May–June 1992

*Unfolding Frankfurt
Aedes Gallery
Berlin, Germany
December 1991

*Fifth International Exhibition of
Architecture at the 1991 Venice Biennale
Venice, Italy
July–August, 1991

Il Tesoro Dell'Architettura
Palazzo Medici-Riccardi
Florence, Italy
March 1990

Snakes and Ladders
Max Protetch Gallery
New York, New York
1989

New York Architecture, 1970–1990
Deutsches Architekturmuseum,
MOPU Gallery
Madrid, Seville, Germany, Moscow
1988

An Architecture of Absence
Contemporary Arts Center
Cincinnati, Ohio
October 1986–January 1987

***Moving Arrows, Eros, and Other Errors:
An Architecture of Absence**
John Nichols Gallery
New York
April–June 1986

***Moving Arrows, Eros, and Other Errors**
The Architectural Association
London
February–March 1986

La Casa Domestica
XVII Triennale
Milan, Italy
January 1986

***Le Affinita'Elettive**
XVI Triennale
Milan
December, 1985

**Nerot Mitzvah: Contemporary Ideas
for Light in Jewish Ritual**
"The Beginning, the End, and the
Beginning Again: A Menorah"
The Israel Museum
September–October 1985

***Third International Architectural
Biennale**
Venice, Italy
July–August 1985

**The Critical Edge: Controversy in Recent
American Architecture**
Zimmerly Museum, Rutgers University
New Brunswick, New Jersey
March–June 1985

***Fin d'Ou T Hou S**
Architectural Association Exhibition
London, England
1985

Cite Un Seen I
Architeckturmuseum
Frankfurt, West Germany
1984

Internationale Bauausstellung
Berlin, West Germany
1984

**Beyond Utopia: Changing Attitudes
in American Architecture**
Film
Michael Blackwood Productions
Museum of Modern Art
New York, New York
December 1983

***Follies: Architecture for the Late
Twentieth Century Landscape**
Leo Castelli Gallery
New York, New York
October–November 1983

***At Home with Architecture**
Mandeville Art Gallery, University
of California
San Diego, California
1983

***Correspondencias**
Palacio de las Alhajas
Madrid, Spain
1982

***Milan Triennale**
Milan, Italy
1982

Model Works of Architects
Contemporary Art Centre
Geneva, Switzerland
Nouveau Musee, Lyons, France
1982

***Trends in Contemporary Architecture**
National Gallery, Alexander Soutzos
Museum
Athens, Greece
1982

***Autonomia Americana, Eisenman/
Hejduk**
Stichting Architectuur Museum
Amsterdam, Holland
1981

***A Decade of Drawings**
Venice Biennale
Venice, Italy
1980

***Autonomous Architecture**
Harvard University
Fogg Museum
Cambridge, Massachusetts
1980

***Houses for Sale**
Leo Castelli Gallery
New York, New York
1980

***10 Immagini per Venezia**
Venice and Rotterdam
1980

***Assonometria**
Antonia Jannone
Milan, Italy
1979

***Assenza-Presenza**
Bologna, Italy
1978

***Numerals**
New Haven, Connecticut
1978

***Abraham, Eisenman, Hejduk, Rossi**
New York, New York
1977

House X
Princeton, New Jersey
1977

*200 Years of American Architectural Drawing
New York, New York
1977

*Biennale Di Venezia
Venice, Italy
1976

*Five Architects
Naples, Italy
1975

The New York Five
Art Net
London, England
1975

Five Architects
Princeton University, School of Architecture
Princeton, New Jersey
1974

Another Chance for Housing: Low-Rise Alternatives
Museum of Modern Art
New York, New York
1973

Birch Burdette Long Memorial Drawing Competition
Architectural League
New York, New York
1973

*Contemporanea
Rome, Italy
1973

*Triennale XV
Milan, Italy
1973

Younger New York Architects
Columbia University
New York, New York
1971
Boston Architectural Center
Boston, Massachusetts
1972

*Architecture of Museums
Museum of Modern Art
New York, New York
1968

*The New City: Architecture and Urban Renewal
Museum of Modern Art
New York, New York
1968

*Forty Under Forty
Architectural League
New York, New York
1966

White, Silver, Grey
University of California at Los Angeles
California
1974

Bibliography

*Indicates major critical writings

Books and Articles by Peter Eisenman

"Aspiring to Disagree: Report of the Jury, Twenty-Second Awards Program." *Progressive Architecture* (Stamford, Connecticut, January 1975), pp. 42–65. (Transcription of the jury's comments, including Peter Eisenman as juror.)

Cities of Artificial Excavation: The Work of Peter Eisenman, 1978–1988. New York: Rizzoli International Publications/Montreal: Centre Canadien d'Architecture, 1994. (A catalog for the exhibition of the same name at the Centre Canadien d'Architecture, May 2 to June 19, 1994.)

Eisenman, Peter (guest co-editor). "The City as Artifact." *Casabella* (special issue, nos. 359–60, Milan, November/December 1971), cover (in Italian and English).

Eisenman, Peter (guest editor with Robert A.M. Stern). "White and Gray: Eleven Modern American Architects." *Architecture + Urbanism* (no. 52, Tokyo, April 1975), pp. 25–180 (in Japanese; English summary pp. 2–4).

*Eisenman, Peter (with Jeff Kipnis and Nina Hofer). *Fin D'ou T Hou S*, Folio IV. London: The Architectural Association, 1985.

*Eisenman, Peter et al. *Recente Projecten — Peter Eisenman Recent Projects*. Nijmegen, The Netherlands: SUN Publishing Co., 1989 (in Dutch and English, edited by Arie Graafland).

Eisenman, Peter with Anthony Vidler and Raphael Moneo. *The Wexner Center for the Visual Arts: Ohio State University*. New York: Rizzoli International Publications, 1989.

Eisenman, Peter. "A Review of Alison and Peter Smithson's *Ordinariness and Light*." *Architectural Forum* (vol. 133, New York, May 1971), pp. 76–80.

Eisenman, Peter. "Aratacism: On the Theoretical Ruins of Arata Isozaki." *Arata Isozaki: Works 30: Architectural Models, Prints, Drawings*. Rikuyo-sha Publishing, Inc., Tokyo, 1992, pp. 186–97 (in Japanese and English).

Eisenman, Peter. "Architecture and the Problem of the Rhetorical Figure." *Architecture + Urbanism* (special feature on Eisenman/Robertson Architects, no. 202, Tokyo, July 1987), cover, pp. 17–22 (in Japanese and English). (Travelers Financial Center, pp. 23–32; Firehouse for Engine Co. 233, pp. 33–48; IBA Social Housing, Berlin, pp. 49–70; Tableware, Calendar, Hardware, Jewelry, pp. 71–80.)

*Eisenman, Peter. "Architecture and the Return of Ornamentation." *Architecture + Urbanism* (no. 211, Tokyo, April 1988), pp. 11–14 (in Japanese).

Eisenman, Peter. "Architecture as a Second Language: The Limits of Representation." Unpublished manuscript, 1985.

Eisenman, Peter. "Architecture as a Second Language: The Texts of Between." In Marco Diani and Catherine Ingraham (eds), *Threshold: Restructuring Architectural Theory*. Evanston: Northwestern University Press, 1989, pp. 69–73. (Reprinted from *Threshold, Journal of The School of Architecture, University of Illinois at Chicago*.)

*Eisenman, Peter. "Architecture as a Second Language: The Texts of Between." *Threshold: Journal of the School of Architecture, University of Illinois at Chicago* (vol. IV, Illinois, Spring 1988), pp. 71–5.

Eisenman, Peter. "Architettura Concettuale: dal Livello Percettivo della Forma ai Suoi Significati Nascoti." In *Contemporanea, Incontri Internazionali d'Arte*. Florence: STIAV Press, 1973, pp. 317–19. (Catalog for the exhibition, in Italian and English; Italian translation of "Notes on Conceptual Architecture.")

*Eisenman, Peter. "Architettura e figura retorica." *Eidos* (no. 1, Asolo, 1987), pp. 12–19. (Italian translation by Fabio Nonis of "Architecture and the Problem of the Rhetorical Figure.")

Eisenman, Peter. "Arquitectura Concettuale: Dal Livello Percettivo della Forma ai Suoi Significati Nascoti." *Casabella* (no. 386, Milan, February 1974), pp. 25–7. (Italian translation of "Notes on Conceptual Architecture II"; in Italian and English.)

Eisenman, Peter. "Aspects du Modernism: La Maison Domino ou le Signe Autoreferentiel." *Les Cahiers de la Recherche Architecturale 12* (Paris, November 1982), pp. 58–65. (French translation of "Aspects of Modernism: The Maison Domino and the Self-referential Sign.")

*Eisenman, Peter. "Aspects of Modernism: Maison Dom-ino and the Self-Referential Sign." *Oppositions 15/16* (Cambridge, Winter/ Spring 1980), pp. 119–28, and *Arsenale Editrice* (Venezia: 1989).

Eisenman, Peter. "Banff Transcripts." *Section A* (vol. 2, nos. 3/4, Montreal, September, 1984), pp. 20–6.

*Eisenman, Peter. "Behind the Mirror: On the Writings of Philip Johnson." *Oppositions 10* (Cambridge, Fall 1977), pp. 1–13.

Eisenman, Peter. "Biology Center for the J.W. Goethe University of Frankfurt, Frankfurt am Main, 1987." *Assemblage* (no. 5, Cambridge, February 1988), pp. 29–50.

Eisenman, Peter. "Blue Line Text." *Deconstruction: Omnibus Volume*. New York: Rizzoli International Publications, 1989, pp. 150–1. (Reprinted from *Architectural Design: Contemporary Architecture*.)

Eisenman, Peter. "Cannaregio." *IAUS Catalog 3: Idea as Model* . New York: Rizzoli International Publications, 1981, p. 120.

Eisenman, Peter. "Cardboard Architecture." *Architecture and Urbanism* (no. 11, Tokyo, November 1973), pp. 185–9.

Eisenman, Peter. "Cardboard Architecture: House I." (Non-published text, August 15, 1972.)

Eisenman, Peter. "Castelli di Carte: Due Opere di Peter Eisenman." *Casabella* (no. 374, Milan, February 1973), pp. 17–31 (Italian translation of "Houses of Cards", in Italian and English).

Eisenman, Peter. "Castillos de Romeo y Julieta." *Arquitectura 270* (Madrid, January/ February 1988), pp. 66–79 (in Spanish).

Eisenman, Peter. "CHORA L WORKS." *Arquitectura 270* (Madrid, January/February 1988), pp. 53–65 (in Spanish).

Eisenman, Peter. "Como casas de naipes." *El Paseante* (no. 8, Madrid, 1988), pp. 96–109 (in Spanish).

Eisenman, Peter. "Conceptual Architecture II: Double Deep Structure I." *Architecture + Urbanism* (no. 3, Tokyo, March 1974), pp. 83–8.

Eisenman, Peter. "Dall Ogetto alla Relazionita: la Casa del Fascio di Terragni." In L. Ferrario & D. Pastore, *Giuseppe Terragni: La Casa del Fascio*. Rome: Instituto Mides, 1982, pp. 54–8. (Italian translation of "From the Object to Relationship: the Casa del Fascio.")

Eisenman, Peter. "Dall'oggetto alla Relazionalita: la Casa del Fascio di Terragni." *Casabella* (no. 344, Milan, January 1970), pp. 38–41. (Italian translation of "From Object to Relationship: The Casa del Fascio.")

Eisenman, Peter. "Das Carnegie Mellon Research Institute: Uberlegungen des Architekten." *Archithese* (Zurich, February 1989), pp. 31–6.

Eisenman, Peter. "Das Guardiola–Haus: Uberlegungen des Architekten." *Archithese* (1:89, Zurich, January/February 1989), pp. 21–5 (in German, translated by Simon Hubacher).

*Eisenman, Peter. "Das Symbol." In *Das Neue Berlin*. Berlin: Gebr. Mann Verlag, 1987, pp. 86–90 (in German).

Eisenman, Peter. "Divisions of Excess: The Emptiness of Hiromi Fujii."

Eisenman, Peter. "El Fin de lo Clasico: El Fin del Comienzo, El Fin del Fin." *Arquitecturas Bis* (Barcelona, March 1984), pp. 29–37. (Spanish translation of "The End of the Classical.")

Eisenman, Peter. "En Terror Firma: Auf den Faehrten der Grotexte." *Archithese* (1:89, Zurich, January/February 1989), pp. 29–30 (in German). (Translation of "En Terror Firma: In Trails of Grotextes.")

Eisenman, Peter. "En Terror Firma: In Trails of Grotextes." *Deconstruction: Omnibus Volume*. New York: Rizzoli International Publications, 1989, pp. 152–3. (Reprinted from *Form, Being, Absence*.)

*Eisenman, Peter. "En Terror Firma: In Trails of Grotextes." *Form, Being, Absence/ Architecture and Philosophy: Pratt Journal of Architecture* (New York, 1988), pp. 111–21.

Eisenman, Peter. "En Terror Firma: In Trails of Grotextes." In Arie Graafland (ed.), *Recent Projects — Peter Eisenman*. Nijmegen, The Netherlands: SUN Publishing Co., 1989, pp. 19–24 (in Dutch and English).

Eisenman, Peter. "En Terror Firma: In trails of Grotextes." *Architectural Design: Decontructivist Architecture II* (vol. 59, London, 1989), pp. 40–43. (Reprinted from *Form, Being, Absence*.)

Eisenman, Peter. "Fin d'Ou T Hou S." In *Follies: Architecture for the Late Twentieth Century Landscape*. New York: Rizzoli International Publications, 1983, pp. 54–6. (Catalog from exhibition at Leo Castelli Gallery.)

Eisenman, Peter. "Fin d'Ou T Hou S." In *Follies: Arquitectura Para el Paisaje de Finales del Siglo XX*. Madrid: MOPU Arquitectura, 1984, pp. 54–7. (Spanish translation.)

Eisenman, Peter. "Firehouse for Engine Company 233, Ladder Company 176, Brooklyn, New York." *Architectural Design 54* (London, November/December 1984), pp. 14–15.

Eisenman, Peter. "Folding in Time: The Singularity of Rebstock." In Greg Lynn (ed.), *Folding in Architecture*. Architectural Design Profile No. 102. London: Academy Group Ltd./Architectural Design, 1993, pp. 22–5. (Rebstockpark Master Plan, Alteka Office Building, Center for the Arts, pp. 26–35.)

*Eisenman, Peter. "From Golden Lane to Robin Hood Gardens; Or If You Follow the Yellow Brick Road, It May Not Lead to Golder's Green." *Architectural Design* (vol. 42, no. 9, London, September 1972), pp. 557–73, 588–92, and *Oppositions 1* (Cambridge, September 1973), pp. 27–56.

*Eisenman, Peter. "From Object to Relationship II: Giuseppe Terragni." *Perspecta 13–14 : The Yale Architectural Journal* (Cambridge: MIT Press, 1971), pp. 36–75.

Eisenman, Peter. "Genuinamente Ingles: la Destruction de la Caja." *Arquitectura* (no. 211, Madrid, March/April 1978), pp. 54–71. (Spanish translation of "Real and English: Destruction of the Box.")

Eisenman, Peter. "Giuseppe Terragni: Casa Giuliani-Frigerio, Como." *Lotus 42* (Milan, 1984), pp. 69–71 (in Italian and English).

Eisenman, Peter. "Hollein's Cave(at): The Haas Haus." *Architecture + Urbanism* (Tokyo, January 1992), pp. 122–3 (in English and Japanese).

Eisenman, Peter. "House El Even Odd." *Architecture + Urbanism* (no. 123, Tokyo, December 1980), pp. 96–8 (in Japanese and English).

Eisenman, Peter. "House II." *IAUS Catalog 3: Idea as Model*. New York: Rizzoli International Publications, 1981, pp. 34–5.

*Eisenman, Peter. "House III: To Adolph Loos and Bertolt Brecht." *Progressive Architecture* (Stamford, Connecticut, May 1974), p. 92.

Eisenman, Peter. "House VI." *Progressive Architecture* (Stamford, Connecticut, June 1977), pp. 57–9.

Eisenman, Peter. "House VI: Frank Residence." Text for catalog and exhibition *Houses for Sale* at the Leo Castelli Gallery. New York: Rizzoli International Publications, 1980, pp. 172–6.

*Eisenman, Peter. "House VI: The Frank Residence." *GA Document Special Issue: 1970– 1980* (Tokyo, 1980), pp. 172–3 (in Japanese and English).

Eisenman, Peter. "House X." *At Home with Architecture: Contemporary Views of the House*. San Diego: Mandeville Art Gallery, 1983, pp. 18–21 (catalog).

Eisenman, Peter. "House X." *IAUS Catalog 3: Idea as Model*. New York: Rizzoli International Publications, 1981, pp. 82–3.

Eisenman, Peter. "Il Futuro della Tradizione: Una Ricerca di *Perspecta 12*, 'Rivista Minore'." *Casabella* (no. 345, Milan, February 1970), pp. 28–33. (Italian translation of "The Big Little Magazine.")

Eisenman, Peter. "Il Wexner Center for Visual Arts a Columbus, Ohio." In Pippo Ciorra (ed.), *Botta, Eisenman, Gregotti, Hollein: musei* (Milano, 1991), pp. 65–81, cover (in Italian).

Eisenman, Peter. "In My Father's House are Many Mansions." *IAUS Catalog 12: John Hejduk: Seven Houses*. New York: Rizzoli International Publications, 1980, pp. 8–20.

Eisenman, Peter. "In Zeit einfalten: Die Singularitat des Rebstock-Gelandes." *Frankfurt Rebstockpark: Folding in Time*. Munich: Prestel-Verlag/Frankfurt: Deutsches Architekturmuseum, 1992 (in German). (Catalog for the exhibition of the Rebstockpark Master Plan project at the Deutsches Architekturmuseum in Frankfurt.)

Eisenman, Peter. "Indicencies: In the Drawing Lines of Tadao Ando." *Tadao Ando: Details*. Yukio Futagawa (ed.), Tokyo: A. D. A. Edita, 1991, pp. 6–9. (in Japanese and English).

*Eisenman, Peter. "It Signifies Nothing … It Is All Dissimulation." Unpublished manuscript, 1985.

*Eisenman, Peter. "L'inizio la fine e poi di nuovo l'inizio-alcune osservazioni sull'idea di scaling." In Gabriella Belli e Franco Rella (eds), *La Citta' e le Forme*. Milan: Mazzotta, pp. 93–8 (in Italian).

Eisenman, Peter. "La Ciudad de la Excavacion Artificial." *Arquitectura* (Madrid, January/February 1984), pp. 42–3. (Spanish translation of "The City of Artificial Excavation.")

Eisenman, Peter. "La Ciudad de la Excavacion Artificial." *Arquitecturas Bis* (Barcelona, December 1983), pp. 21–3. (Spanish translation of "The City of Artificial Excavation.")

Eisenman, Peter. "La Futilidad de los Objectos." *Arquitectura* (Madrid, January/ February 1984), pp. 33–56. (Spanish translation of "The Futility of Objects.")

Eisenman, Peter. "La Maison Dom-ino e il Segno Autoreferenziale." *Sulle Trace di Le Corbusier*. San Marco: Arsenale Press, 1989, pp. 21–35.

Eisenman, Peter. "Laboratorios in Frankfurt." *Arquitectura 270* (Madrid, January/February 1988) (in Spanish).

*Eisenman, Peter. "Le Rappresentazioni del Dubbio: Nel Segno del Segno." *Rassegna 9* (Milan, March 1982), pp. 69–74 (in Italian); also "The Representations of Doubt: At the Sign of the Sign." *Rassegna 9,* (English original, unpaginated).

*Eisenman, Peter. "Lecturas de MiMESis: Malinterpretadas no Significan NADA." *Mies Van der Rohe: Su Architectura v Sus Discipulos*. Madrid: La Direccion General para la Vivienda y Arquitectura, 1987, pp. 92–104. (Exhibition catalog. Spanish translation of "miMISes READING: does not mean A THING", German version.)

Eisenman, Peter. "Meier's Smith House: Letter to the Editor." *Architectural Design*. (London, August 1971), p. 520.

*Eisenman, Peter. "Metaphysics, Mystique, and Power." *AA Files* (no. 12, London, Summer 1986), p. 107. (A review of John Hejduk's *Mask of Medusa*.)

*Eisenman, Peter. "miMISes READING: does not mean A THING." In *Mies Reconsidered: His Career, Legacy. and Disciples.* Chicago: Art Institute of Chicago/New York: Rizzoli Publications, 1986, pp. 86–98 (catalog).

*Eisenman, Peter. "miMISes READING: does not mean A THING." *Mies van der Rohe: Vorbild und Vermaechtnis.* Frankfurt: Deutsches Architekturmuseum, pp. 85–95. (Exhibition catalog. German translation of "miMISes READING: does not mean A THING.")

*Eisenman, Peter. "Misreading Peter Eisenman." *Houses of Cards.* New York: Oxford University Press, 1987, pp. 167–86.

Eisenman, Peter. "Modern Architecture 1919–1939: Polemics." Princeton University Library, 1968 (catalog with introduction and annotations for an exhibition of architectural books; unpublished).

*Eisenman, Peter. "Moving Arrows, Eros and Other Errors." *Arquitectura* (no. 270, Madrid, January/February 1988), pp. 67–81 (in Spanish and English). (Reprinted from *The Culture of Fragments.*)

*Eisenman, Peter. "Moving Arrows, Eros and Other Errors." *The Culture of Fragments,* Precis 6. New York: Columbia Graduate School of Architecture, Planning and Preservation, Spring 1987, pp. 139–43.

*Eisenman, Peter. "Moving Arrows, Eros and other Errors." *Chiasmos II: Strategier* (Copenhagen, December 1988), pp. 29–32. (Danish translation by Carsten Juel-Christiansen.)

Eisenman, Peter. "Moving Arrows, Eros, and Other Errors: An Architecture of Absence." III Architectural Biennale, Venice, 1985. (Original text to accompany exhibition panels.)

Eisenman, Peter. "Moving Arrows, Eros, and Other Errors: An Architecture of Absence." *SD* (special feature on Peter Eisenman, Tokyo, March 1986), pp. 53–7. (Japanese translation of text for Venice Biennale.)

Eisenman, Peter. "Notes on a Conceptual Architecture." *Formalism, Realism, Contextualism* (Tokyo, 1979). (Japanese translation of "Notes on a Conceptual Architecture.")

Eisenman, Peter. "Notes on Conceptual Architecture IIA." *Environmental Design Research Association* (vol. II, Stroudsburg, Pennsylvania, 1973), pp. 319–22.

Eisenman, Peter. "Notes on Conceptual Architecture IIA." *On Site* (no. 4, New York, 1973), pp. 41–4.

Eisenman, Peter. "Notes on Conceptual Architecture: Towards a Definition." *Casabella* (nos. 359–360, Milan, November/December 1971), pp. 48–58 (in Italian and English).

*Eisenman, Peter. "Notes on Conceptual Architecture: Towards a Definition." *Design Quarterly* (special double issue, nos. 78–9, 1970), pp. 1–5, cover.

Eisenman, Peter. "Oltre Lo Sguardo: L'Architettura nell'Epoca dei Media Elettronici." ("Visions' Unfolding: Architecture in the Age of Electronic Media.") *Domus* (Milan, January 1992), pp. 17–24 (in Italian and English).

Eisenman, Peter. "Peter Eisenman." *Der Postmoderne Salon: Architekten uber Architecten* (Berlin, 1991), pp. 88–95.

Eisenman, Peter. "Peter Eisenman." *Yale Seminars in Architecture* vol. 2. New Haven: Yale University Press, 1982, pp. 49–87.

Eisenman, Peter. "Peter Eisenman: The Affects of Singularity." *A.D.* (vol. 62, November/December 1992)

Eisenman, Peter. "Post-Functionalism." *Arquitecturas/Bis 22* (Barcelona, 1978), pp. 6–12. (Spanish translation of "Postfunctionalism.")

*Eisenman, Peter. "Post-Functionalism." *Oppositions 6* (Cambridge, Fall 1976), pp. i–iii (editorial).

*Eisenman, Peter. "Post/EI Cards: A Reply to Jacques Derrida." *Assemblage* (no. 12, Cambridge, August 1990), pp. 14–17.

Eisenman, Peter. "Postfunktionalismus." In Gerald R. Blomeyer & Barbara Tietze, *Opposition zur Moderne: Aktuelle Positionen in der Architekur.* Weisbaden: Friedr. Vieweg & Sohn Verlagsgesellschaft, 1980. (German translation of "Post-Functionalism.")

*Eisenman, Peter. "Real and English: Destruction of the Box I." *Oppositions 4* (Cambridge, May 1974), pp. 5–34.

Eisenman, Peter. "Recent Works." *Architectural Design: Deconstruction II* (no. 1/2, London, 1989), pp. 40–61.

*Eisenman, Peter. "Representations of the Limit: Writing a 'Not Architecture'." In Daniel Libeskind, *Chamberworks: Architectural Meditations on Themes from Heraclitus.* London: Architectural Association Folio, 1983, pp. 6–8.

Eisenman, Peter. "Residence, Critique of Weekend House by Philosopher, Sociologist, and Architect Himself." *Progressive Architecture* (Stamford, Connecticut, June 1977), pp. 57–67.

Eisenman, Peter. "Roosevelt Island Competition." *Controspazio* (no. 4, Rome, December 1975), pp. 30–1.

*Eisenman, Peter. "Sandboxes: House 11a." *Architecture + Urbanism* (special issue, no. 112, Tokyo, January 1980), pp. 221–4, cover (in Japanese and English).

Eisenman, Peter. "Semiotica e Architettura (la Casa del Fascio), *Casabella* (Milan, October, 1977), p. 25 (in Italian and English).

Eisenman, Peter. "Shore Birds, or The Rocket's Red Glare." Introduction to Brad Collins & Diane Kasprowicz (eds), *Gwathmev Siegel: Buildings and Projects 1982–1992.* New York: Rizzoli International Publications, 1993, pp. 4–13.

Eisenman, Peter. "Sports of Our Climate." *New York Times* (July 16, 1983), opposite editorial page.

Eisenman, Peter. "Stadium Ghosts." *New York Times* (April 2, 1980), opposite editorial page.

*Eisenman, Peter. "Strong Form, Weak Form." *Architecture in Transition: Between Deconstruction and New Modernism.* Munich: Prestel, 1991, pp. 33–45 (in German and English).

*Eisenman, Peter. "TEXt AS Zero, or The Destruction of Narrative." In Lars Lerup, *Planned Assaults.* Centre Canadienne d'Architecture/MIT Press, 1987, pp. 93–8.

*Eisenman, Peter. "The Authenticity of Difference: Architecture and the Crisis of Reality." *Center: A Journal for Architecture in America, University of Texas at Austin* (vol. 4, New York, 1988), pp. 50–7.

Eisenman, Peter. "The Author's Affect: Passion and the Moment of Architecture." *Anyone* (New York, 1991) pp. 200–11.

Eisenman, Peter. "The Author's Affect: Passion and the Moment of Architecture." *Critical Space* (June 1992), pp. 213–19 (in Japanese). (Translation of English text published in *Anyone.*)

Eisenman, Peter. "The Beginning, the End, and the Beginning Again." *Nerot Mitzvah: Contemporary Ideas for Light in Jewish Ritual.* Catalog for the Israel Museum, Jerusalem, 1986, p. 62.

*Eisenman, Peter. "The Beginning, the End, and the Beginning Again: Some Notes on an Idea of Scaling." *SD* (special issue on Peter Eisenman, Tokyo, March 1986), pp. 6–7, cover (in Japanese).

Eisenman, Peter. "The Big Little Magazine: *Perspecta 12* " and "The Future of the Architectural Past." *Architectural Forum* (vol. 131, no. 3, New York, October 1969), pp. 74–5, 104.

Eisenman, Peter. "The Blue Line Text." *Architectural Design: Contemporary Architecture.* (London, January/February 1989), pp. 6–9.

Eisenman, Peter. "The Carnegie Mellon Research Institute." *GA Documents 23* (Tokyo, April, 1989), pp. 82–4.

Eisenman, Peter. "The City as Memory and Immanence." *Zone* (Toronto 1986), pp. 440–1.

Eisenman, Peter. "The City as Memory and Immanence." *Zone* (vol. 1, New York, Fall 1985), pp. 440–1.

Eisenman, Peter. "The City of Artificial Excavation." (Extract) *Architectural Design Profile* (London, 1983), pp. 24–7.

*Eisenman, Peter. "The City of Artificial Excavation." *Architectural Design* (London, nos. 1–2, January 1983), pp. 91–3.

Eisenman, Peter. "The End of the Classical." *Montana State University Architectural Review* (vol. 3, Bozeman, Montana, Spring 1984), pp. 2–11. (Reprinted from *Perspecta 21.*)

*Eisenman, Peter. "The End of the Classical." *Perspecta 21: The Yale Architectural Journal* (Cambridge, Summer 1984), pp. 154–72.

Eisenman, Peter. "The End of the Classical: The End of the Beginning, the End of the End." *Chiasmos II: Strategier* (Copenhagen, December 1988), pp. 9–21. (Danish translation by Carsten Juel-Christiansen.)

Eisenman, Peter. "The Futility of Objects." *Harvard Architecture Review* (vol. 3, Cambridge, Winter 1984), pp. 65–82.

*Eisenman, Peter. "The Futility of Objects." *Lotus 42* (Milan, February 1984), pp. 63–75. (A condensed version of "The Futility of Objects" in Italian.)

*Eisenman, Peter. "The Graves of Modernism." *Oppositions 12* (Cambridge, Spring 1978), pp. 36–41.

*Eisenman, Peter. "The House of the Dead as the City of Survival." *IAUS Catalog 2: Aldo Rossi in America: 1976–1979.* New York: Institute for Architecture and Urban Studies, 1979, pp. 4–15 (introduction).

*Eisenman, Peter. "The Houses of Memory: The Texts of Analogy." Introduction to Aldo Rossi, *The Architecture of the City.* Cambridge: MIT Press, 1982, pp. 3–12.

Eisenman, Peter. "The OSU Center for the Visual Arts" and "Fin D'ou T Hou S." *Architectural Design* (vol. 55, nos. 1/2, London, January 1985), pp. 44–55.

Eisenman, Peter. "The Story of AND O." *Tadao Ando: The Yale Studio & Current Works.* New York: Rizzoli International Publications, 1989, pp. 137–9.

Eisenman, Peter. "Three Texts for Venice." *Domus* (no. 611, Milan, November 1980), pp. 9–11, cover (in Italian and English).

Eisenman, Peter. "Towards an Understanding of Form in Architecture." *Architectural Design* (London, October 1963), pp. 457–8.

*Eisenman, Peter. "Transformations, Decompositions and Critiques: House X." *Architecture + Urbanism* (special issue, no. 112, Tokyo, January 1980), pp. 14–151, cover (in Japanese and English).

Eisenman, Peter. "Unfolding Events: Frankfurt Rebstockpark and the Possibility of a New Urbanism." *Unfolding Frankfurt.* Berlin: Ernst & Sohn, 1991, pp. 8–17 (in German and English).

Eisenman, Peter. "University Art Museum, California State University, Long Beach, California." *GA Document 18: GA International '87* (Tokyo, April 1987), pp. 13–15.

Eisenman, Peter. "University Campus, Long Beach, California: The Museum Rediscovered." *Lotus 50* (Milan, 1986), pp. 128–35 (in Italian and English).

Eisenman, Peter. "Vioes que se desdobram: A arquitetura na Epoca da Midia Eletronica." *Oculum 3* (Sao Paulo, March, 1993), pp. 14–22 (in Portuguese and English).

Eisenman, Peter. "Wettbewerbsprojeckt Rebstock in Frankfurt, 1991." *Werk, Bauen + Wohnen* (March 1992).

Eisenman, Peter. "Yale Seminars in Architecture, Peter Eisenman." *Architecture + Urbanism* (no. 166, Tokyo, July 1984), pp. 19–26. (Japanese translation of Yale Seminars in Architecture.)

Eisenman, Peter. "Zum Forshungsinstut der Carnegie Mellon Universitat und der Verwaltungsgebaude der Oxford Development Company." *Dekonstruktion? Dekonstructivismus?...* (Lengerich, 1990), pp. 110–16.

*Eisenman, Peter. *House X.* New York: Rizzoli International Publications, 1982.

*Eisenman, Peter. *Houses of Cards.* New York: Oxford University Press, 1987.

Eisenman, Peter. Introduction to *Writings* by Philip Johnson. New York: Oxford University Press, 1979, pp. 10–25. (Edited version of "Behind the Mirror.")

*Eisenman, Peter. *La Fine del Classico.* Venice: Cluva, 1987. (Italian translations of essays and articles. Introduction by Franco Rella, postscript by Renato Rizzi, translated by Renato Rizzi and Daniela Toldo.)

*Eisenman, Peter. *Moving Arrows. Eros, and Other Errors: An Architecture of Absence,* Box 3. London: The Architectural Association, 1986.

Eisenman, Peter. Preface to *IAUS Catalog 3: Idea as Model.* New York: Rizzoli International Publications, 1981, p. 1.

*Eisenman, Peter. *The Formal Basis of Modern Architecture.* Dissertation for the Degree of Doctor of Philosophy. Cambridge: University of Cambridge, 1963 (unpublished).

Eisenman, Peter. *The Ohio State Center for the Visual Arts Competition.* New York: Rizzoli International Publications, 1984.

Frankfurt Rebstockpark: Folding in Time. Munich: Prestel-Verlag/Frankfurt: Deutsches Architekturmuseum, 1992 (in German). (A catalog for the exhibition of the Rebstockpark Master Plan at the Deutsches Architekturmuseum in Frankfurt.)

La Diversitat Cultural en el Dialeg Nord-Sud. Barcelona: Departament de Cultura de la Generalitat de Catalunya/Institut Catala de Bibliografia, 1991, pp. 111–14 (in Catalan).

Peter Eisenman & Frank Gehry. New York: Rizzoli International Publications, 1991. (A catalog for the Fifth International Exhibition of Architecture at the 1991 Venice Biennale.)

Unfolding Frankfurt. Berlin: Ernst & Sohn, 1991 (in German and English). (A catalog for the exhibition of Rebstockpark project at Aedes Gallery, Berlin.)

Forthcoming Books

Eisenman, Peter (with Jacques Derrida and Jeff Kipnis). *CHORA L WORKS.* London: Architectural Association.

*Eisenman, Peter. *Giuseppe Terragni: Transformations, Decompositions, Critiques.* New York: Rizzoli International Publications.

Rakatansky, Mark (ed.). *Collected Essays of Peter Eisenman.* Princeton, NJ: Princeton Architectural Press, 1994.

Articles on Eisenman Architects

"A Skyscraper For A Post-Phallic Age." *Harper's Magazine* (July 1993), p. 12.

Abrams, Janet. "Misreading Between the Lines." *Blueprint* (no. 14, London, February 1985), pp. 16–17.

"Am Rebstock soll eine neue Trabantenstadt entstehen." *Wiesbadener Kurier* (December 13, 1992) (in German).

American Institute of Architecture, New York Chapter. "Nunotani Headquarters Building", "Center for the Arts." *New York Architecture Volume 6.* New York: AIA New York Chapter, 1993, pp. 9, 14–15, 35, 38–39.

Anderson, Kurt. "A Crazy Building in Columbus: Peter Eisenman, Architecture's

Bad Boy, Finally Hits His Stride." *Time* (November 20, 1989).

"Anything Goes." *New Criterion* (New York, January 1992), pp. 2–3.

"Architektur Ist Ein Schwaches Medium." *Taz Hamburg* (Hamburg, July 7, 1992), p. 19 (in German).

"Arquitecto americano expoe maquetes exoticas no Masp." *Folha de S. Paulo* (May 18, 1993), Section D, p. 3.

Armaly, Fareed. "Plan." *Intelligente Ambiente II* (1994), pp. 50–67.

Baird, George. "The Return of Peter Eisenman." *GSD News* (1994), pp. 21–3.

"BAC Craft Awards Highlight Craftsmanship." *Bricklayers and Allied Craftsman* (February 1993).

"Bahnhof Friedrichstrasse." *Lotus 80* (1994), pp. 118–22.

Barris, Roann. "Eisenman and the Erosion of Truth." *20/1 Art & Culture* (School of Architecture & Design, University of Illinois at Chicago, 1:1, Spring 1990), pp. 20–37.

Beckelmann, Jurgen. "Der Optimismus der Architekten." *Frankfurter Rundschau* (December 12, 1992).

Benjamin, Andrew (ed.). *Re:Working Eisenman*. London: Academy Editions/Ernst & Sohn, 1993.

Benson, Robert. "Convention." *Inland Architect* (July/August 1993), pp. 53–8.

Benson, Robert. "Eisenman's Architectural Challenge." *New Art Examiner* (Summer 1990), pp. 27–30.

Benson, Robert. "Wexing Eloquent in Columbus." *Inland Architect* (May/June 1990), pp. 34–43, cover.

"Berlin's Reinhardt Homage: Why Not Eisenman?" *International Herald Tribune* (December 1992) pp. 19–20.

"Berlin: A New Twist." *ARTnews* (April 1993).

Bischoff, Michael. "Warum Le Corbusier die Welt nicht verandert hat." *Frankfurter Allgemeine Zeitung* (January 4, 1992).

Blackford, Darris. "Architect, Critics Give Convention Center High Marks." *Columbus Dispatch* (February 27, 1993).

Blackford, Darris. "Great Expectations Convention Center's Curtain Going Up." *Columbus Dispatch* (February 28, 1993).

Blackford, Darris. "Open House Draws Crowd." *Columbus Dispatch*

Blackford, Darris. "Those Who Built It Like the Center." *Columbus Dispatch* (February 28, 1993), p. 1.

Bletter, Rosemary Haag. "Five Architects — Eisenman, Graves, Gwathmey, Hejduk, Meier." *Journal of the Society of Architectural Historians* (New York, May 1979), pp. 205–7.

Blundo, Joe. "If the New Convention Center Were a House ..." *Columbus Dispatch* (March 7, 1993).

Bottiger, Helmut. "Wider das Kunstfeindliche Subentionstheater." *Frankfurter Rundschau* (Frankfurt, July 29, 1992).

Bouw, Matthjis "Peter Eisenman — Towards a Supple Geometry." *Wiederhall 16* (1993), pp. 40–55.

Campbell, Robert. "The Fascinating and Abstract World of Peter Eisenman." *Boston Globe* (May 27, 1986), p. 67.

Castro, Ricardo. "Cryptic Philosophy, New Direction in Architecture." *Gazette* (Montreal, March 1994), p. 2

"Center's Architecture Draws International Recognition." *Columbus Dispatch* (March 7, 1993), pp. 70, 86.

Ciorra, Pippo (ed.). *Peter Eisenman: opere e progetti*. Serie Documenti di Architettura, no. 71. Milan: Electa, 1993.

"College of Design, Architecture, Art and Planning, University of Cincinnati, Ohio." *Zodiac 7* (Milan, March/August 1992), pp. 96–109 (in English and Italian).

Color of an Artist: Haus Immendorff. Hamburg: Artfound Print Co./Galerie fur Architektur Renate Kammer und Angelika Hinrichs, owners, 1993 (in German and English). (A catalog for the exhibition of the Haus Immendorff project at Galerie fur Architektur Renate Kammer und Angelika Hinrichs, Hamburg.)

Colquhoun, Alan. "The Competition for the Center for the Visual Arts at Ohio State University." *The Ohio State Center for the Visual Arts Competition*. New York: Rizzoli International Publications, 1984, pp. 132–5.

"Convention Center Earns Foundation Award." *Columbus Dispatch* (October 8, 1993).

Cooleybeck, Patrick and John Abela. "Do It For Van Gogh." *Dimensions: Journal of University of Michigan College of Architecture* (vol. 6, Ann Arbor, 1992), pp. 92–101.

"Costruire L' Impossibile" *Cultura* (November 1992) p. 18.

Cuomo, Alberto. "Architettura e Negativita." *Controspazio* (anno X, Rome, July/August 1978), pp. 42–7 (in Italian).

Dal Co, Francesco. "Ten Architects in Venice." *Architecture + Urbanism* (no. 121, Tokyo, October 1980), pp. 26–33 (in English and Japanese).

Dal Co, Francesco. "Ten Architects in Venice." In *10 Immagini Per Venezia*. Venice: Officina Edizioni, pp. 55–65 (in Italian). (Catalog of the exhibition in Venice, April 1–30, 1980.)

Dannatt, Adrian. "Any Old How." *Building Design* (London, March 6, 1992), p. 14.

Darley, Gillian. "Ideas Sit Heavily on the Wall." (March 15, 1993).

Davidson, Cynthia. "A Game of Eisenman Seeks." *Architecture + Urbanism* (Tokyo, September 1991), pp. 12–13, cover (in Japanese and English).

Davis, Douglas. "Modernism Revisited." *The Ohio State Center for the Visual Arts Competition*. New York: Rizzoli International Publications, 1984.

Davis, Douglas. "The Death of Semiotics (in Late Modern Architecture), the Corruption of Metaphor (in Post-Modernism), the Birth of Punctum (in Neomania)." *Art Forum* (May, 1984), pp. 56–63.

Dawson, Layla. "Peter Eisenman: The Man Who Discovered Folding Architecture." *Pace Magazine* (vol. 47, Hong Kong, October 1992).

de Mendonca, Denise Xavier. "Peter Eisenman — Blue Line Text; Edificio-Sede da Nunotani Toquio, Japoa; Centro de Convencoes, Greater Columbus, Ohio; Concurso Nordliches Derendorf, Dusseldorf, Alemanha"; "Instabilidade e Turbulencia." *Arquitectura e Urbanismo* (April/May 1993), pp. 46–66, cover.

"Del mundo mecanico al electronico." *Arquitectura* (Buenos Aires, December 12, 1992) (in Spanish).

"Der Turmbau am Zirkus." *Frankfurter Allgemeine* (Frankfurt, November 17, 1992), p. 1.

Derrida, Jacques. "A Letter to Peter Eisenman." *Assemblage* (no. 12, August 1990), pp. 7–13.

Derrida, Jacques. "A Letter to Peter Eisenman." *Critical Space* (no. 6, Tokyo, 1992), pp. 98–106 (in Japanese).

Derrida, Jacques. "Why Peter Eisenman Writes Such Good Books." *Architecture + Urbanism: EISENMANAMNESIE* (extra edition, Tokyo, August 1988), pp. 113–24, cover (in Japanese and English). (Translation of the French original in Jacques Derrida, *Psyche: L'invention de l'autre*, Paris: Galilee, 1987, pp. 495–508.)

Derrida, Jacques. "Why Peter Eisenman Writes Such Good Books." In Arie Graafland (ed.), *Peter Eisenman: Recent Projects*, Nijmegen: SUN, 1989, pp. 169–82 (in Dutch and English). (Reprinted from *Architecture + Urbanism: EISENMANAMNESIE*, August 1988, pp. 113–24.)

Derrida, Jacques. "Why Peter Eisenman Writes Such Good Books." In Marco Diani and Catherine Ingraham (eds). *Threshold: Restructuring Architectural Theory.* Evanston: Northwestern University Press, 1989, pp. 99–105. (Reprinted from *Architecture + Urbanism: EISENMANAMNESIE,* August 1988, pp. 113–24.)

di Forti, Massimo. "Costruire l'impossibile." *Il Messaggero* (Rome, November 3, 1992), p. 18 (in Italian).

Dibar, Carlos L. "La deconstruccion de Nunotani: Un edificio de oficinas en Tokio." *El Cronista Arquitectura & Disegno* (Buenos Aires, December 2, 1992), pp. 1–2, 8, cover (in Spanish).

"Die Ordnung Des Scheinbar Regellosen." *Frankfurter Allgemeine Zeitung* (December 1993).

Doubilet, Susan. "The Divided Self." *Progressive Architecture* (March 1987), pp. 81–92, cover. (Berlin, Travelers, Artifacts.)

"Dusseldorf: der Kunstier Bau." *Ambiente* (Munich, October 1993), p. 18 (in German). (Haus Immendoff)

Dyer Szabo, Brenda. "Contrasti e Armonia: An Alliance of Oppositions." *Habitat Ufficio* (no. 58, Milan, June/July 1992), pp. 50–9 (in Italian and English).

Egelkraut, Ortrun. "Flurstuck Am Zirkus 1." *Berliner Zeitung* (Berlin, November 16, 1992) (in German).

Egelkraut, Ortrun. "Planung ohne Grund." *Berliner Zeitung* (Berlin, December 18, 1992) (in German).

"Ein neuer Stadtteil am Rebstock." *Gallus Drehscheibe* (February 1993) (in German).

"Ein Projekt im Namen Max Reinhardt." *Der Tages Spiegel* (Berlin, July 29, 1992) (in German).

"Eisenman diz que Sao Paulo tem perfil do seculo 20." *Folha de S. Paulo* (May 19, 1993), p. 2.

"Eisenman und Rebstock." *Arkitektur* (April 1992) (in German).

Eisenman, Peter. "People Who Live in Glass Houses Should Not Throw Stones." In Color of An Architect: Peter Eisenman, Haus Immendorff, Hamburg: Artfound Print Co./Galerie fur Architektur Renate Kammer und Angelika Hinrichs, owners, 1993, pp. 2–11, (in German and English).

"Eisenman, Provocador." *Folha de S. Paulo* (May 19, 1993), p. 17.

"Er Labt Wande Explodieren." *Hamburger Abendblatt* (Hamburg, June 30, 1992) (in German).

Evans, Robin. "Not to Be Used for Wrapping Purposes — Peter Eisenman: Fin d'Ou T Hou S." *AA Files* (London, Autumn 1985), pp. 68–78.

"Excavating Eisenman." *Architecture* (June 1994), pp. 57–63.

"Experimentos arquitectonicos." *Arquitectura* (Buenos Aires, January 23, 1993), p. 6.

"Experimentos arquitectonicos." *Arquitectura* (Buenos Aires, January 23, 1993) (in Spanish).

"Falten Statt Hamburger." *Hamburger Morgen Post* (Hamburg, July 2, 1992) (in German).

"'Faltungen' auf Rebstockgelande." *Frankfurter Allgemeine Zeitung* (Frankfurt, December 16, 1992) (in German).

Filho, Antonio Goncalves. "Masp abriga a polemica arquitectura de Eisenman." *Folha de S. Paulo* (May 17, 1993), Section 4, p. 8.

Filler, Martin. "Peter Eisenman: Polemical Houses." *Art in America* (vol. 68, no. 9, New York, November 1980), pp. 126–33.

Findsen, Owen. "Exhibit Spotlights Architects' Designs for DAAP, Disney." *Cincinnati Enquirer.*

Fischer, Adelheid. "Towers of Power." *Express* (Memphis, Summer 1992), pp 21–5.

Forster, Kurt. "Eisenman/Robertson's City of Artificial Excavation." *Archetype* (vol. 2, no. 2, Melbourne, Spring 1981), pp. 84–5.

Forster, Kurt. "Monuments to the City." *Harvard Architectural Review* (Spring 1984), pp. 107–21.

Forster, Kurt. "Traces and Treason of a Tradition." *The Ohio State Center for the Visual Arts Competition.* New York: Rizzoli International Publications, 1984, pp. 135–40.

Fox, Catherine. "Emory's Sights Set Clearly on World-Class Arts Facility." *Atlanta Journal* (Living Section, Atlanta, October 9, 1992).

Frampton, Kenneth. "Apropos Eisenman." *Domus* (no. 688, Milan, September 1987) (in Italian and English).

Frampton, Kenneth. "Eisenman Revisited: Running Interference." *Architecture + Urbanism: EISENMANAMNESIE* (extra edition, Tokyo, August 1988) pp. 57–69, cover (in Japanese and English). (Reprinted from *Domus,* no. 688, September 1987.)

Frampton, Kenneth. "Zabriskie Point: The Somnambulist Trajectory." *Casabella* (nos. 586/587, Milan, January/February 1992), pp. 8–13 (in Italian).

Frederic Levrat. "Peter Eisenman." *L'Architecture d'Aujourd'hui* (no. 279, Paris, February 1, 1992), pp. 98–115, cover (in French and English).

Freedman, Adele. "Turning Architecture from the Sun toward the Moon." *Toronto Globe & Mail* (February 23, 1993), p. C13.

Fuji, Hirome. "From Conception to Decomposition." *Architecture + Urbanism* (no. 112, Tokyo, January 1980), pp. 249–52 (in Japanese and English).

Galloway, David. "Berlin's Reinhardt Homage: Why Not Eisenman?" *International Herald Tribune* (December 19–20, 1993), p. 18.

Galloway, David. "Berlin's Reinhardt Homage: Why Not Eisenman?" *International Herald Tribune* (nos. 19/20, December 1992), p. 16.

Gandelsonas, Mario. "From Structure to Subject." *Oppositions 17* (Cambridge, Summer 1979), pp. 6–29.

Gandelsonas, Mario. "From Structure to Subject: The Formation of an Architectural Language." In Eisenman, Peter, *House X.* New York: Rizzoli International Publications, pp. 7–31.

Gandelsonas, Mario. "Linguistics in Architecture." *Casabella* (no. 374, Milan, 1973), pp. 17–30 (in Italian and English).

Gandelsonas, Mario. "On Reading Architecture." *Progressive Architecture* (vol. 53, March 1972), pp. 68–88.

Gass, William. "House VI." *Progressive Architecture* (June 1977), pp. 60, 62, 64.

Ghirardo, Diane. "Peter Eisenman: il Camouflage dell'avanguardia." *Casabella* (1994), pp. 22–7.

Gilson, Nancy. "Buildings that Challenge." *Columbus Dispatch* (Arts Section, June 3, 1992).

Giovannini, Joseph, "Greater Convention Center." *Domus 750* (June 1993), pp. 25–33.

Giovannini, Joseph. "Beyond Convention." *Architecture* (May 1993), pp. 52–63, cover.

Gironnay, Sophie. "L'archeologie fictive revele la pensee et les aeuvres souvent troublantes de Peter Eisenman; Le Deconstructivisme." *Le Devoir* (1994), p. C1.

Gironnay, Sophie. "Provocateur et Architecte." *Le Devoir* (1994).

Giurgola, Romaldo. "Five on Five: the Discreet Charm of the Bourgeoisie." *Architectural Forum* (vol. 138, no. 4, May 1973), pp. 46–57.

Glusberg, Jorge. "Centro Wexner." *Projeto* (no. 163, Buenos Aires, 1993), pp. 50–3.

"Go to Venice and See the Whole World." *Independent* (London, September 11, 1991).

Goldberger, Paul. "A Remembrance of Visions Pure And Elegant." *New York Times* (January 3, 1993), Section 2, p. 29.

Goldberger, Paul. "Architecture's 'Big Five' Elevate Form." *New York Times* (November 26, 1973), p. 33.

Goldberger, Paul. "The Museum that Theory Built." *New York Times* (Arts and Leisure Section, November 5, 1989), pp. C1, C38.

Graafland, Arie. "Decentering van Structuraliteit in het Ontwerp — Peter Eisenman's Decompositie." *Esthetische Theorie en Ontwerp: Architectuur. Macht en Lichaam* (Delft, Uitgeverij SUN, November 1984), pp. 213–32, cover (in Dutch).

Graafland, Arie. "Peter Eisenman: Architecture in absentia." In Arie Graafland (ed.), *Peter Eisenman: Recent Projects,* Nijmegen: SUN, 1989, pp. 95–126 (in Dutch and English).

Green, Jonathan. "Algorithms for Discovery." *The Wexner Center for the Visual Arts, The Ohio State University.* New York: Rizzoli International Publications, 1989, pp. 28–31.

Gregory, Anne. "New Convention Center Makes Sense." *Upper Arlington News* (Arlington, November 11, 1992).

Griddings, Scalings, Tracings and Foldings in the Work of Peter Eisenman. Sao Paulo: Editora Pini, Ltda, 1993 (in Portuguese and English). (A catalog for the exhibition of the same title at the Museu de Arte de Sao Paulo, Brazil.)

Gutman, Robert. "House VI." *Progressive Architecture* (June 1977), pp. 57–67.

Hacker, Marc. "With a Certain Laughter and Dance." *Investigation in Architecture/Eisenman Studios at the GSD: 1983–85.* Cambridge: Harvard Graduate School of Design, 1986, pp. 26–42.

Hales, Linda. "American Architects at Venice Biennale." *Washington Post* (Washington, DC, September 19, 1991).

Hallett, Joe. "Columbus Beholds Unconventional Center." *The Blade* (Toledo, February 28, 1993), p. 3.

Heller, Fran. "New York Architect Finds Responsive 'Home' in Ohio." *Cleveland Jewish News* (October 30, 1992), pp. 42–3.

Henderson, Justin. "Unconventional Wisdom." *Interiors* (June 1993), pp. 82–5.

"Hochkonjunktur Der Hochhausprojekte." *Gallus Drehscheibe* (1993).

Hofer, Nina. "Fin d'Ou T Hou S." *Architectural Follies.* New York: Leo Castelli Gallery, October 22 – November 19, 1983.

Huxtable, Ada Louise. "The Troubled State of Modern Architecture." *New York Review of Books* (May 1, 1980), pp. 22–9.

Irace, Fulvio. "Eisenman House VI: Architettura di Geometrie Visibili/Analysis of Eisenman's House VI." *MODO* (no. 12, Milan, September 1978), pp. 27–31 (in Italian).

Janik, Detlev. "Die Ordnung des Scheinbar Regellosen." *Frankfurter Rundschau* (September 11, 1993).

Jansen, Karin. "Manege frei: Peter Eisenman." *Die Wochenschau,* Wettbewerbe.

Jencks, Charles. "The Perennial Architectural Debate, The Eisenman Paradox: Elitism, Populism and Centrality." *Architectural Design Profile.* London: 1983, pp. 4–23.

Jencks, Charles. *Post Modern Architecture,* revised edition. London: Academy Editions, 1978, pp. 8, 64, 66, 100, 101, 118, 121, 122, 126, 127.

Jodidio, Philip, (ed.). *Contemporary American Architects.* Cologne: Benedikt Taschen GmbH, 1993, pp. 56–61 (in English, German, French). (Wexner Center for the Arts, Columbus Convention Center.)

Jodidio, Philip. "Jour de Cristal." *Connaissance des Arts* (April 1993), pp. 59–63.

Johnson, Philip. "Philip Johnson on Eisenman and Gehry." *Architectural Design* (London, January/February 1992), pp. 26–31.

Johnson, Philip. "Philip Johnson on Peter Eisenman." *Architecture + Urbanism: EISENMANAMNESIE* (extra edition, Tokyo, August 1988), pp. 9–11, cover (in Japanese and English).

Johnson, Philip. Introduction to *Peter Eisenman and Frank Gehry.* New York: Rizzoli International Publications, 1991, pp. 2–3. (Catalog for the Fifth International Exhibition of Architecture at the 1991 Venice Biennale.)

Kahn, Eve M. "New From the Deconstructivist Guru." *Wall Street Journal* (May 12, 1993), p. A12.

Kamin, Blair. "America's Oddest Architect." *Chicago Tribune* (April 19, 1993), Section 13 (Sunday Arts), cover, pp. 4–5, 28.

Kipnis, Jeffrey. "Architecture Unbound: Consequences of the Recent Work of Peter Eisenman." *SD* (special issue on Peter Eisenman, Tokyo, March 1986), pp. 26–33 (in Japanese and English).

Kipnis, Jeffrey. "Star Wars III: The Battle at the Center of the Universe." *Investigation in Architecture/Eisenman Studios at the GSD: 1983–85.* Cambridge: Harvard Graduate School of Design, 1986, pp. 42–7.

Kipnis, Jeffrey. "The Law of ana-. On Choral Works." In Arie Graafland (ed.), *Peter Eisenman: Recent Projects,* Nijmegen: SUN, 1989, pp. 145–60 (in Dutch and English).

Kipnis, Jeffrey. "The Ohio State University Center for the Visual Arts and the Architecture of Modification." *Casabella* (488/9, Milan, January/February 1984), pp. 96–9 (in English).

Kitayama, Kirjo. "Peter Eisenman Tokyo, Koizumi Sangyo and Nunotani Headquarters." *Lotus 76,* pp. 87–95.

Klemmer, Clemens. "Gefaltete Architektur." *Neue Burcher Zeitung* (September 19, 1992), p. 9 (in German).

Krauss, Rosalind. "Death of a Hermaneutic Phantom: Materialization of the Sign in the Work of Peter Eisenman." *Architecture + Urbanism* (no. 112, Tokyo, January 1980), pp. 189–219.

Krauss, Rosalind. "Death of a Hermeneutic Phantom: Materialization of the Sign in the Work of Peter Eisenman." In Peter Eisenman, *Houses of Cards,* New York: Oxford University Press, 1987, pp. 166–84.

Kwinter, Sanford. "Der Genius Der Materie: Projekt Fur Cincinnati." *Arch +* (December 1993).

Kwinter, Sanford. "The Genius of Matter: Eisenman's Cincinnati Project." In *Peter Eisenman and Frank Gehry.* New York: Rizzoli International Publications, 1991, pp. 8–9. (Catalog for the Fifth International Exhibition of Architecture at the 1991 Venice Biennale.)

Lacy, Bill. "Peter Eisenman Building — Before and After Earthquake." *Architectural Record* (New York, January 1992), p. 48 (cartoon).

Lauer, Heike. "Living and Working at Rebstockpark." *Archigrad 1/1992: Planning and Building on the 50th Parallel* (Frankfurt, 1992), pp. 37–41.

LeCuyer, Annette. "Designs on the Computer." *Architectural Review* (January 1995), pp. 76–9.

Lemos, Peter. "The Triumph of the Quill." *Village Voice* (May 3, 1983), pp. 96, 99.

Lerup, Lars. "House X by Peter Eisenman." *Design Book Review* (San Francisco, Summer 1983), pp. 44–8.

Levesque, Luc. "Le theatre desoperation pliable: Concours de circonstances ..." *Inter art actuel* (vol. 53, Quebec, 1992), pp 34–7 (in French).

Libeskind, Daniel. "Peter Eisenman and the Myth of Futility." *Harvard Architectural Review* (vol. 3, Winter 1984), pp. 61–4.

Libeskind, Daniel. "The Lamentable Center: A Response to Peter Eisenman." Unpublished article, 1984.

Litt, Steven. "Daring Design Shouts Gotcha!" *Plain Dealer* (Cleveland, April 25, 1993).

Litt, Steven. "Eisenman on Design." *Plain Dealer* (Cleveland, October 28, 1992).

Litt, Steven. "Exhibit Explores Master Architects' Visionary Works." *Plain Dealer* (September 20, 1992).

"Living Room." *Architecture* (August 1992), p. 101.

Lubowski, Bernd. "Heimkehr und spate Versohnung ." *Berliner Morgenpost* (Berlin, July 29, 1992) (in German).

Lubowski, Bernd. "Senat sperrt sich gegen Max-Reinhardt-Museum." *Berliner Morgenpost* (Berlin, November 12, 1992) (in German).

Lubowski, Bernd. "Making shop drawings with the spirit of Japanese craftmanship." *Nikkei Architecture* (Tokyo, February/March 1992), pp. 254–8 (in Japanese).

Ludlow, Randy. "Columbus Proud of New Lady." *Cincinnati Post* (March 3, 1993).

Lynn, Greg (guest editor). "Rebstock Park Masterplan", "Alteka Office Building", "Center for the Arts, Emory University." In *Folding in Architecture,* Architectural Design Profile no. 102. London: Academy Group Ltd, 1993, pp. 26–35.

MacLeod, Douglas. "ACS Kompendium '93." (November 1993).

Macrae-Gibson, Gavin. "The Anxiety of the Second Fall: House El Even Odd, Peter Eisenman." In *The Secret Life of Buildings: An American Mythology for Modern Architecture.* Cambridge: MIT Press, 1985, pp. 30–51.

Maier, Susanne. "Hausverbot im Theater sienes Vaters!" *B.Z.* (July 29, 1992), p. 32 (in German).

"Manhattan Waterfront Design Project: Peter Eisenman and Michael Graves." In *The New City: Architecture and Urban Renewal.* New York: Museum of Modern Art, 1967, pp. 36–41. (Catalog including Manhattan Waterfront design project with Michael Graves.)

Maruyama, Hiroshi. "Of a mis-Leading, for a mis-Leading." *SD* (special issue on Peter Eisenman, Tokyo, March 1986), pp. 7–8 (in Japanese and English).

"Max Reinhardt Monument Challenges 'Business as Usual'." *Architectural Record* (March 1993).

McGuigan, Cathleen (with Maggie Malone). "Stone, Steel and Cyberspace." *Newsweek* (February 27, 1995), p. 73.

Mendini, Alessandro. "Dear Peter Eisenman." *Domus* (no. 611, Milan, November 1980), p. 1 (editorial, in Italian and English).

Merkel, Jayne. "Looking for the Future: The Center for the Visual Arts Competition at Ohio State University." *Inland Architect* (December 1983), pp. 110–16.

Mitarheiter, N.Z. & Petersohn, Harlmut. "Ein City-Kristall mit Signatur des Jahrhunderts." (Berlin, December 12, 1982) p. 20 (in German).

Mitarheiter, N.Z. & Petersohn, Harlmut. "Nach oben ist der Alex offen." (November 18, 1992) (in German).

Mitarheiter, N.Z. & Petersohn, Harlmut. "Nunotani Building." *Nikkei Architecture* (no. 442, Tokyo, September 1992), pp. 206–11 (in Japanese).

Mitarheiter, N.Z. & Petersohn, Harlmut. "Nunotani Building." *Shinkenchiku* (67:10, Tokyo, October 1992), pp. 187–206 (in Japanese).

Moenninger, Michael. "Die geplants Unordnung." *Frankfurter Allgemeine Zeitung* (February 22, 1993).

Moenninger, Michael. "Marke Eigenbau: Der Architekt Peter Eisenman." *Frankfurter Allgemeine Magazin* (Heft 681, March 19, 1993), pp. 14–23, cover (in German).

Mollard, Beth. "Nightmare on High Street: Center's Design Causes Delay." *Columbus Dispatch* (Columbus).

Moneo, Rafael. "Unexpected Coincidences." In *The Wexner Center for the Visual Arts, The Ohio State University.* New York: Rizzoli International Publications, 1989, pp. 40–5.

Moore, Rowan. "Eisenman Plays the Centre Forward." *Blueprint* (April 14, 1993), p.14.

Muschamp, Herbert. "This Time, Eisenman Goes Conventional." *New York Times* (March 2, 1993).

Nasar, Jack. "Convention Center's Interior an Exciting Space." *Columbus Dispatch* (March 14, 1993), p. 5C.

Newkirk, Margaret. "Our Strange New Convention Center: Haute or Hoot?" *The Other Paper* (Columbus, November 12–18, 1992), cover.

Newkirk, Margaret. "News Notes." *Oculus* (55:4, December 1992).

"No Construyo Solo Edificios; Construyo Ideas." *El Pais* (November 1993).

"Nunotani Building." *Japan Architect 9* (January 1993), pp. 150–3 (in Japanese and English).

"Ohio State University Center for the Visual Arts." *Section A* (vol. 2, no. 2, Montreal, April/May 1984), pp. 22–5.

Paschke, Regina. "Viel Ehre mit Profit." *Die Tageszeitung* (Berlin, July 29, 1992) (in German).

"Pastel City Tinged with Menace." *Globe and Mail* (March 1994), pp. 14, 15.

Pelissier, Alain. "Peter Eisenman: L'Espace Autre." *Techniques et Architecture* (vol. 360, Paris, June/July 1985), pp. 26–55 (in French).

Perrella, Stephen. "Columbus Convention Center Opens." *Newsline,* Columbia University Architecture, Planning, Preservation (New York, March/April 1993), p. 8.

"Peter Eisenman Il Progetto Del Vuoto." *Risk* (1994), p. 19.

"Peter Eisenman in Buenos Aires." *Clarin Arquitectura* (special supplement, Buenos Aires, December 5, 1992), pp. 1–5, cover.

"Peter Eisenman." *Archimade* (no. 44, June 1994), pp. 5–31.

"Peter Eisenman: Emory Center For the Arts." *GA International 36* (Tokyo, 1993), pp. 32–3.

"Peter Eisenman: Max Reinhardt Haus, Berlin." *AA Files 25* (London, March 1993), pp. 8–13.

"Peter Eisenman; Oltre lo sguardo." *Domus* (no. 734, Milan, January 1992), pp. 17–24 (in Italian and English).

"Peter, los filosofos y tambien los criticos." *Arquitectura* (Buenos Aires, December 12, 1992).

Pinon, Helio. "La Forma de la Forma." *Arquitectura de los Neovanguardias* (Barcelona, 1984), pp. 117–65 (in Spanish).

Pione, Carolyn. "Columbus Convention Center 'Not Your Typical Box'." *Cincinnati Enquirer* (April 11, 1993), p. D-5.

Pione, Carolyn. "Columbus Convention Center: New Frontier in Architecture?" *Alliance Review* (March 11, 1993), p. 12, cover.

Pommer, Richard. "The New Architectural Supremacists." *Artforum* (vol. 15, no. 2, October 1976), pp. 38–43.

Pontbriand, Chantal. *Parachute.* Revue D'Art Contemporain Inc., 1993.

Post, Nadine. "Cockeyed Optimism in Columbus." *Engineering News-Record* (February 8, 1993), pp. 22–4, 58, cover, editorial.

Post, Nadine. "Throwing Construction A Curve: No More Mister Highbrow." *Engineering News-Record* (June 21, 1993), pp. 24–7, cover.

Rajchman, John. "Perplications" *Critical Space* (no. 6, Tokyo, 1992), pp. 113–29 (in Japanese).

Rajchman, John. "Perplications: On the Space and Time of Rebstockpark." *Unfolding Frankfurt.* Berlin: Ernst & Sohn, 1991, pp. 20–77, (in German and English). (Catalog for the exhibition of the Rebstockpark project at Aedes Gallery.)

"Regenswasser von den Dachern in den Weiher." *Frankfurter Allgemeine Zeitung* (December 9, 1992) (in German).

"Reinhardt-Haus vom Senat abgelehat." *Berliner Zeitung* (November 13, 1992), p.1.

Rella, Franco. "Figure nel labirinto. La matamorfosi di una metafora." In *La Fine del Classico.* Venice, 1987, pp. 9–25.

Riskind, Jonathan. "Convention Center: Beauty or Beast?" *Columbus Dispatch* (July 15, 1992), p. 58.

Robertson, Jaquelin. "Five on Five: Machines in the Garden." *Architectural Forum* (vol. 138, no. 4, May 1973), pp. 46–57.

Rochon, Lisa. "Nunotani's Headquarter Building." *International Contract* (Toronto, May 1993), pp. 46–9.

Roffo, Analia. "La arquitectura no resulve problemas sociales." *Buenos Aires* (February 4, 1993), p. 8.

Rosen, Cheryl. "Columbus Readies Daring New Facility." *Business News Travel* (December 1, 1992), cover.

Runge, Irene. "Konsulat Wachtiger als Schauspielhaus." *Neues Deutschland* (November 13, 1992) (in German).

Salvato, Al. "New 'Gem' to Brighten UC Campus (Architects Praise DAAP Building Plan)." *Cincinnati Post* (June 1994).

Schmidt, Martinus. "Erben fuhlen sich bruskiert." *Neuezeit* (Berlin, November 13, 1992) (in German).

Schubert, Peter. "Krimi um 'Filetgrundstuck'." *Berliner Morgenpost* (Berlin, November 14, 1992) (in German).

Schwarz, Ullrich. "Peter Eisenman: Dazwischen." *Der Architekt* (January, 1993).

Schweitzer, Eva. "150 Meter hoch an der Weidendammer Brucke?" *Berliner Morgenpost* (December 16, 1992) (in German).

Seabrook, John. "The David Lynch of Architecture." *Vanity Fair* (January 1991), pp. 74–9, 125–9.

"Seismische Architektur Das Nunotani Building in Tokio." *Architektur, Innenarchitektue. Technischer Ausbau* (Leinfelden-Echterdingen, Germany: Verlagsanstalt Alexander Koch GmbH, April, 1993), pp. 36–9.

Sola-Morales , Ignasi de. "Del Objeto a la Dispersion: Arquitectura Artificialis. Proyecto de Peter Eisenman para le Friedrichstrasse de Berlin." *Arquitecturas/Bis 42* (Barcelona, December 1983), pp. 16–21 (in Spanish).

Sola-Morales, Ignasi de. "Cuatro Notas Sobre la Arquitectura Reciente de Peter Eisenman." *El Croquis* (41, Madrid, December 1989), pp.16–23, cover (in Spanish and English).

Sola-Morales, Ignasi de. "Peter Eisenman: Arquitectura del Presente." *La Vanguardia* (Barcelona, September 16, 1986), p. 33 (in Spanish).

Solomon, Nancy B. "Flexible Theaters." *Architecture* (August 1992), pp. 95–102.

Somol, R.E. "O-O." *Progressive Architecture* (special issue on Eisenman/Wexner Center, October 1989), p. 88, cover.

Somol, R.E. "Peter Eisenman: Wexner Center for the Visual Arts, Columbus/ Ohio." *Domus* (Milan, January 1990), pp. 38–47 (in Italian and English).

Somol, Robert. "Accidents Will Happen." *Architecture + Urbanism* (Tokyo, September 1991), pp. 4–7, cover (in Japanese and English).

Sorkin, Michael. "Architecture: Solid Geometry: Coming off a Theoretical Tangent, Architect Peter Eisenman Puts a New Spin on Design." *House and Garden* (October 1989), pp. 62–6.

Speicher, Stephan. "Baukunst und Investorengluck." *Frankfurter Allgemeine Zeitung* (December 12, 1992) (in German).

Stache, Rainer. "Aus fur dieses haus? Schade!" *Berliner Morgenpost* (December 16, 1992) (in German).

Stein, Jerry. "CAC Salutes 'Superstar' Architects." *Cincinnati Post* (April 4, 1992), p. 7B.

Steinhausen, Ansgar. "Zwischen Stadtautobahn und Gleisanlagen." *Badische Zeitung* (January 18, 1993), p. 11.

Tafuri, Manfredo. "Les Bijoux Indiscrets." Introduction to *Five Architects NY.* Rome: Officina Edizioni, 1976, pp. 7–34. (Introduction to Italian translation.)

Tafuri, Manfredo. "Meditations of Icarus." Unpublished manuscript. (Later published in Eisenman, Peter, *Houses of Cards,* New York: Oxford University Press, 1987, pp. 167–87.)

Tafuri, Manfredo. "Peter Eisenman: The Meditations of Icarus." In Peter Eisenman, *Houses of Cards,* New York: Oxford University Press, 1987, pp. 167–87.

Taki, Koji. "Dialogue on Peter Eisenman." *Architecture + Urbanism* (no. 112, Tokyo, January 1980), pp. 245–48 (in Japanese and English).

Taylor, John. "Mr. In-Between, Deconstructing with Peter Eisenman." *New York Magazine* (October 17, 1988), pp. 46–52.

Taylor, Mark. "Eisenman's Coup." *Progressive Architecture* (special issue on Peter Eisenman, October 1989), p. 89, cover.

Terrahe, Antje. "In Raum und Zeit entFalten: Wohnraum schaffen, ohne ins Umland zu Wuchern." *Frankfurter Rundschau* (December 12, 1992), p. 8 (in German).

"The 39th Annual P/A Awards: Architectural Design Award, Alteka Office Building." *Progressive Architecture* (January 1992), pp. 63–5.

"The 40th Annual Progressive Architecture Design Citation, Center for the Arts." *Progressive Architecture* (January 1993), pp. 78–81.

"The Site Report—Nunotani Tokyo NC Building." *Nikkei Architecture* (3:2, Tokyo: 1992), pp. 254–8 (in Japanese).

"Tokio Scragerklotz." *Ambiente* (January/ February 1993), p. 20.

Trelstad, Julie M. "Convention Center Breaks Convention." *I.D.* (March/April 1993), p. 19.

"Turning Architecture from the Sun to the Moon." *Globe and Mail* (February 1993), p. C13.

"Un progetto per Siena: Il concorso internazionale per piazza matteotei — la Lizza." Bernardo Secchi & Chiara Merlini (eds), Milan: Electa, 1992, pp. 80–5 (in Italian and English).

"Una Scomposta Nervrosi." *Architettura* (March 1993), p. 32.

Unger, Oscar. "Ein neuer Stadtteil zeischen Autobahn und Rebstockweiher." *Frankfurter Neue Presse* (December 9, 1992) (in German).

"Unspeakable or Unreadable." *Blueprint* (no. 84, London, February 1992), p. 12. (Review of *Anyone.*)

Vallongo, Sally. "Columbus Exhibition Contrasts Top Architects." *The Blade* (July 19, 1992).

van Dijk, Hans. "Autonomia Americana. Eisenman/Hejduk." *Wonen TA/BK* (21/22, Hilversun, The Netherlands, 1981) (in Dutch). (Catalog of the exhibition at the Stichting Architectuur Museum.)

van Dijk, Hans. "Eisenman/Hejduk: Architectuur Halverwege Amerika en Europa." *Wonen TA/BK* (21/22, Hilversun, The Netherlands, November 1980), pp. 7–10 (in Dutch).

van Dijk, Hans. "Peter Eisenman en het Berlangan Naar de Klassieke Rede." ("Peter Eisenman and the Desire for Classical Reason.") *Wonen TA/BK* (Hilversun, The Netherlands, February 1977), pp. 4–10 (in Dutch).

"Verjungende Falten." *Taz Hamburg.* (July 2, 1992), p. 19 (in German).

Vidler, Anthony. "After the End of the Line." *Architecture + Urbanism: EISENMANAMNESIE* (extra edition, Tokyo, August 1988), pp. 147–61, cover (in Japanese and English).

Vidler, Anthony. "Counter-Monuments in Practice: The Wexner Center for the Visual Arts." In *The Wexner Center for the Visual Arts, The Ohio State University.* New York: Rizzoli International Publications, 1989, pp. 32–8.

Vidler, Anthony. *The Architectural Uncanny: Essays in the Modern Unhomely.* Cambridge, Massachusetts: MIT Press, 1992.

"Warum Le Corbusier Die Welt Nicht Verandert Hat." *Ereignisse Und Gestalten* (January 1992).

Weibel, Peter. "Intelligente Wesen in Einem Intelligenten Universum." *Intelligente Ambiente* (1994), pp. 6–26.

"Wettbewerbsprojekt Rebstock in Frankfurt." *Werk, Bauen + Wohnen* (Frankfurt, March 1992), pp. 36–9 (in German).

"Wexner Center for the Visual Arts." *Museo d'arte e architectura.* Lugano: Edizioni Charta s.r.l., 1992, pp. 94–101. (Catalog for the exhibition at the Museo Cantonale d'arte.)

"What's On In February & March Halls of Fame." *Elle Decor* (February/March 1993).

Whiteman, John. "Site Unseen — Notes on Architecture and the Concept of Fiction: Peter Eisenman: Moving Arrows, Eros and Other Errors." *AA Files* (no. 12, London, Summer 1986), pp. 76–84.

Wise, Michael Z. "Reinhardt's Restitution." *Forward* (New York, February 26, 1993), pp. 1, 11.

Wise, Michael. "United Berlin Divided Over Its 'Eiffel Tower'." *Los Angeles Times* (March 29, 1993), pp. F1, F9.

Witte, Joachim. "Droht Zweite Enteignung Max Reinhardt?" (November 13, 1992) (in German).

Wittmann, Jochen. "Konkurrenz fur das Brandenburger Tor." *Der Standard Immobilien* (January 7, 1933), p. 1.

Wurm, Fabian. "Elogen auf Eisenman." *Baumeister* (February 1993).

Yatsuka, Hajime. "The Adventure in the Labyrinth of the Knight for Purity." *SD* (special issue on Peter Eisenman, Tokyo, March 1986), pp. 70–1 (in Japanese and English).

Zellner, Lisa K. "Convention Center Group Takes Show On Road." *Upper Arlington News* (Arlington, November 4, 1992).

Zohlen, Gerwin. "Im Dienst der Erben." *Suddeutsche Zeitung* (December 12, 1992) (in German).

Zuck, Barbara. "Vision Serves Geldin Well as Director of Wexner Center." *New York Times* (June 1994), p. 2B.

Acknowledgments

The work in this book was made possible:

through the efforts of my staff, including particularly Richard Rosson, Sergio Bregante, Setu Shah, Cynthia Davidson, Diano Ibrahim, Megan McFarland, Bernadette Latour, Megan McFarland, Benedicte Mioli, Rudolph Kammeri, and Alexander Wiedemann;

through all the Clients who commissioned this work; and

through the co-operative efforts of Engineers and Consultant.

We would like to thank The Images Publishing Group, Paul Latham, and Alessina Brooks for their invitation to participate in this monograph series.

Photography Credits

Dick Frank Studio
House, I, House II, House III, House IV, House VI, Cannaregio Town Square, Madison Components Plant, Romeo and Juliet Castles, Tokyo Opera House, Biocentrum, La Villette, Carnegie Mellon Research Institute, Guardiola House, Aronoff Center for Design and Art, Koizumi Sangyo Office Building, Siena Bank Competition, Banyoles Olympic Hotel, Cooper Union Housing, Atocha 123 Hotel, Rebstockpark Master Plan, Alteka Office Building, Emory Center for the Arts, Max Reinhardt Haus, Nordliches Derendorf Master Plan, Haus Immendorff

Ron Forth
Aronoff Center for Design and Art

David Morton
House III

D.G. Olshavasky/ARTOG
Wexner Center for the Visual Arts and Fine Arts Library, Greater Columbus Convention Center

Jeff Goldberg/ESTO
Fuller/Toms Loft, Wexner Center for the Visual Arts and Fine Arts Library, Greater Columbus Convention Center

Jochen Littkemann
Max Reinhardt Haus

Mark C. Schwarts
Progressive Corporation Office Building

Masao Ueda
Koizumi Sangyo Office Building

Michael Moral
University Art Museum

Reingard Gorner
IBA Social Housing

Shigwo Ogawa/Shinkenchiku
Nunotani Office Building

Van der Vlugt & Claus
Groningen Music-Video Pavilion

Wolfgang Hoyt/ESTO
Firehouse for Engine Company No 233 and Ladder Company No 176, Travelers Financial Center

Rendering Credits

Ed Keller/*Straylight Imaging*
Max Reinhardt Haus

Index

Bold page numbers refer to projects
included in Selected and Current Works.

Every effort has been made to trace the original source of copyright material contained in this book.
The publishers would be pleased to hear from copyright holders to rectify any errors or omissions.

The information and illustrations in this publication have been prepared and supplied by Eisenman Architects.
While all reasonable efforts have been made to ensure accuracy, the publishers do not, under any circumstances,
accept responsibility for errors, omissions and representations express or implied.